D1433710

16
8
DD

654540

Choosing and Using Educational Software:
A Teachers' Guide

To Deirdre and Derek

Choosing and Using Educational Software:
A Teachers' Guide

David Squires
and
Anne McDougall

Routledge
Taylor & Francis Group

LONDON AND NEW YORK

UK   RoutledgeFalmer, 11 New Fetter Lane, London EC4P 4EE
USA   RoutledgeFalmer, Taylor & Francis Inc., 325 Chestnut Street,
8th Floor, Philadelphia, PA 19106

First Published 1994 by the Falmer Press

Reprinted 2002, 2003
By RoutledgeFalmer

Transferred to Digital Printing 2003

RoutledgeFalmer is an imprint of the Taylor & Francis Group

**A catalogue record of this publication is available from the British
Library**

ISBN 0 7507 0306 7 cased
ISBN 0 7507 0307 5 paper

**Library of Congress Cataloging-in-Publication Data are available
on request**

Jacket design by Caroline Archer

Typeset in 11/13pt Garamond by
Graphicraft Typesetters Ltd., Hong Kong

Printed in Great Britain by Hobbs the Printers Ltd, Totton, Hants

Contents

Contents

About the Authors

David Squires has been a secondary teacher in England. In 1978 he joined the staff of the Advisory Unit for Microtechnology in Hatfield, and subsequently worked as an Adviser for Computers in Education for Devon. In 1983 he joined the staff of the Computers in the Curriculum Project, King's College, University of London, later becoming a director of this project with responsibility for science, and a Lecturer in Educational Computing within the Centre for Educational Studies, King's College. His main research interests are in the design and evaluation of educational software and the use of IT-assisted information systems to support research.

Anne McDougall has worked as a secondary teacher in Australia and then as a computer programmer in the USA. In 1973 she took up a research fellowship in computer education at the University of Melbourne, developing software for use in undergraduate teaching. Her subsequent lecturing and research work has been concerned with computers and learning at secondary and primary school levels. She has lectured and published on many aspects of computer use in education, and is now the Senior Lecturer in Educational Computing at Monash University.

David Squires and Anne McDougall met in 1981 at an international conference on educational computing. In the following years they have collaborated on a number of projects, including the presentation of a regular Master of Educational Studies course at Monash University on the evaluation and development of educational software. Work for this course has been the basis of the development of the ideas presented in this book.

Preface

Although there have been computers in schools for more than fifteen years now, our understanding of the ways in which they might be used to enhance learning is still very much in its infancy, and the ideas, theoretical frameworks and language needed to think about and discuss the issues in educational computing are still developing.

In this book we reject the traditional checklist approach to selection of software for schools, arguing that this is seriously limited by its focus on attributes of the software at the expense of consideration of educational questions. We propose a new paradigm for thinking about educational software, based on a consideration of the mutual interactions between the perspectives of the major 'actors' in the use of educational software: the student, the teacher and the software designer. This leads to an approach to software selection closely associated with software use, and emphasizing educational considerations such as classroom interactions, theories of learning processes and curriculum issues.

This book aims to assist teachers who are in any way involved in the selection and use of computer software in school settings.

Discussions with our students, at both Monash University and King's College, have contributed a good deal to our formulation of the ideas in the book. Our thanks are also due to Royston Sellman, Deryn Watson, Sophie McCormick, Geoff Cumming, Martin Gomberg, Howard Flavell and Deirdre Squires, who read and commented on draft manuscripts for the book. The support of Monash University while one of the authors (Anne McDougall) was on Outside Studies Programme leave has enabled the collaboration essential for the completion of this book. Without the support of Deirdre Squires and Derek McDougall our task would have been impossible.

1 Educational Software

All teacher training, whether at the pre-service or the in-service stage, should include training in assessing and selecting software. This should be part of the in-depth training in the pedagogical uses of the information technologies which teachers need to supplement the introductory training they usually receive in the operation of microcomputers and in their classroom use. If teachers were given such training, they would be able to convert the potential of computer-based learning into the actuality of instructional use which would meet their objectives and curriculum needs. (OECD, 1989 p. 93)

In this book we reject the traditional checklist approach to the selection of software for education, arguing that this is seriously limited by its focus on attributes of the software at the expense of consideration of educational questions. We propose a new paradigm for thinking about educational software, leading to an approach to software selection closely associated with software use, and emphasizing educational considerations such as classroom interactions, theories of learning processes, and curriculum issues.

Computers and Software in Schools

It would be astonishing indeed if the ubiquity of computer technology in the society outside were not reflected in some way in schools. Despite initial high costs, schools began to introduce computers in the mid-seventies. These initiatives were justified in rather vocational terms with arguments about preparing children for living and working in a computerized society. However, school computer activities, predominantly courses in computer literacy with programming in the BASIC language, or computer awareness considering more social issues related to computer use, bore little relation to computing work outside schools; see for example Bacon (1981) for syllabus guidelines from the British Computer Society Schools Committee, Rogers and Austing (1981) for recommendations of the Elementary and Secondary Schools Subcommittee of the United States Association for Computing Machinery, and McDougall (1980) and Penter (1981) for guidelines from two state Education Departments in Australia. More recently, school computer studies curricula are using software such as word processors, desktop publishing programs, spreadsheets and data bases, partly in an attempt to reflect more closely computing activities in business and industry (see for example Department of Education and Science, 1990; Victorian Curriculum and Assessment Board, 1989).

Quite early the possibility of using computers in the actual teaching process was seen as interesting, and possibly economical (see, for commentary on these early developments, Woodhouse and McDougall, 1986). This led to the development of computer programs to teach, usually by drill and practice or tutorial methods, topics from school curricula: arithmetic skills, foreign language vocabulary, factual geographical or historical material, and so on. It soon became clear that computers could not do nearly as well at teaching as human teachers, and would never replace them. But as skills in the development of educational software and understanding of human-computer interaction developed, the idea that computers could be used to support and enhance learning persisted.

Now microcomputers in schools are commonplace; the discussion has moved from the possibility of a computer in every classroom to the likelihood that quite soon every child who wants one will have a portable computer (National Council for Educational Technology, 1992a). Many teachers and students are using computer-based packages as classroom resources, and computer software is used in a wide range of types of learning activities. The ways in which these packages are used vary with the context of their use, with different age levels, subject areas or classroom settings.

Much of the software used in schools has been written specifically for the purpose; some, as mentioned earlier, is not written for schools, but is used because it suits the aims of teachers and students. For the purposes of this book we shall include as educational software any software that is used in an educational context, whether or not it was specifically designed for educational use. There is enormous variety in the educational software available to schools, so teachers need to have sophisticated skills in software selection.

Evaluation, Review, Selection and Assessment of Software

The terms evaluation, review and selection are all used in the literature on assessment of educational software, though different writers use some or all of these words with slightly different meanings. Sometimes they are used interchangeably, as if they all share one meaning. For example, Langhorne, Donham, Gross and Rehmke (1989) use evaluation and selection synonymously, their text on evaluation being illustrated by a diagram titled with the word selection, and many checklists designed for software selection use evaluation in the titles (see for example Salvas and Thomas, 1984; MicroSIFT, 1982; Reay, 1985). Other writers take care to define what is meant by each of the terms they use (for example Alexander and Blanchard, 1985; Winship, 1988; Preece and Jones, 1985; Miller and Burnett, 1986). However, apart from selection, on the meaning of which all those who use the term appear to agree, their definitions do not always correspond with one another, particularly in the breadth or specificity of meaning of the terms review and evaluation. For example, Johnston (1987) clearly uses the term evaluation to refer to selection of software, but as well explains that

> Evaluation activities may be carried out for several purposes: formative, in improving program design; comparative, to determine a program's instructional effectiveness; direct observation to determine what actually happens when a program is used; and predictive, in evaluating program characteristics. (Johnston, 1987 p. 41)

It would appear that the predictive evaluation used here corresponds to selection in the papers that use the term.

It is important for our purposes to distinguish clearly between selection, review and evaluation, as they are useful terms for discussing the assessment of educational software. We shall establish now the meanings of these terms as they will be used throughout the book.

By *selection* we mean the assessment of software by teachers in anticipation of its use with groups of students in classrooms or with individual students. For practical reasons software selection, as is the case for selection of other types of classroom resources, is usually done without the opportunity of seeing students use the materials. In a sense the notion of software selection is paradoxical; the experiences provided by educational software are totally dependent on the learning and teaching situation in which it is used, yet teachers generally have to choose software packages without actually trying them out, relying on the teacher's personal experience of students and classroom environments to anticipate how the software might be used and how effective it will be.

We shall describe as *reviewing* educational software the process of assessing it to write a summary of its features and characteristics for the information of others who are involved in software selection. In this sense review is a form of selection. To complete a review, the reviewer goes through a process similar to that undertaken during selection, but review is carried out with a much larger and more diverse audience in mind. Reviews can be used as a first step in selection.

Evaluation of software can take place during either the development of the software or the use of a completed package. The aims of these two types of evaluation are slightly different. Formative evaluation, evaluation during development, focuses on possible modifications to the software. Summative evaluation, after publication, is concerned with the quality and variety of experiences that the software can support. In either case the evaluation involves observation of the actual use of the package by students. Both types of evaluation may be carried out by teachers, formative evaluation as trialling for software developers, and summative for purposes such as writing software reviews for publication.

When we quote other writers we shall of course use the words selection, review and evaluation as they have done. However, in the main text of the book we shall make a clear distinction particularly between the processes of selection and evaluation of software, as the two are distinct and different processes, and, as we shall see later, confusing them leads to significant problems in software selection.

We shall use the term *assessment* as a broad term, to describe processes that apply to any or all of selection, review and evaluation of educational software.

Thinking, Talking and Writing about Educational Software

As understanding of classroom use of computers and of learning processes increases, techniques for developing educational software are still evolving. There is a continuing need for teachers to develop skills in software assessment and use (Johnston, 1987; Preece and Jones,

1985; OECD, 1989). Thinking, talking and writing about software are most important in this, and to this end theoretical frameworks have been developed for discussing and examining educational software and issues in its use. Some of the theoretical frameworks are relatively simple, but widely used nevertheless; others are somewhat more complex. These frameworks are examined in some detail in Chapter 6. The area of educational software use is still evolving; we see this book as contributing to this evolution.

Talking with teachers who have experience with the use of computers in classrooms, we hear over and again comments which suggest that better ways of considering educational software are needed. For example, teachers say that the way they use software with their students is often very different from what the designers seem to have intended, although they find it difficult to describe exactly what they mean by this. Others, selecting software, have worked through a long list of review criteria but still do not feel they can express things they know intuitively are important about a software package. Reay (1985) confirms this experience:

> Often the questions teachers would like to have addressed are not addressed. There appears to be a need, therefore, for an approach to evaluating software which is general enough to be widely applicable but specific enough to provide the kind of information that will allow decisions to be made about the acceptability of programs under consideration. This is a need which has been expressed by many teachers the writer has worked with. (Reay, 1985 p. 80)

Comments such as these suggest that the frameworks and terminologies needed for examination and assessment of educational software are not yet sufficiently well developed for clear, effective discussion of the salient issues and ideas.

Scope and Structure of the Book

In this book we propose and discuss a paradigm for thinking, talking and writing about educational software. The paradigm takes account of the most important 'actors' involved in the development and use of educational software — the student, the teacher and the software designer — to ensure a comprehensive and balanced consideration of issues. We shall argue that it assists clarification of ideas for discussing the assessment and use of educational software.

We use the paradigm to discuss and examine concepts that we believe already exist in the minds of many software users and developers, but have not been articulated more widely because there have not been adequate theoretical frameworks with which to describe them. We use the comprehensive viewpoint facilitated by our paradigm to discuss the assessment and use of educational software.

Teachers from different subject areas are likely to have different perceptions of the use of computers in learning, as the knowledge, aims and skills associated with different subjects vary quite widely. These differences are reflected in the popularity of different types of software in different subject areas. Despite these variations there are fundamental issues concerned with designing, assessing and using educational software that transcend subject divisions. In the chapters that follow we shall discuss many of these issues, referring, sometimes briefly, to a wide range of software from a variety of subject areas.

Educational software can be used to support or extend learning experiences within many different educational approaches (see, for example, Shingles, 1988). Teachers who subscribe to a view of education as the acquisition of knowledge in the form of factual information will find there are many computer packages that can be used to support this. Teachers who value learning by discovery or by interaction with other students will find there are various computer-based packages to support these approaches. If learning is regarded as an active process in which students build their own intellectual structures, refining and developing these with time as they encounter new experiences, there are also computer-based materials to support this view. Of course we are simplifying the situation here. Few teachers use a single approach; most use several, adapting as appropriate to different settings and situations. The point is, that whatever the approach taken, software can usually be found to support and enhance that view of learning. In choosing packages to illustrate issues in educational computing we have included software intended to support a wide variety of teaching approaches and theories of learning.

We base our commentary and argument on our experiences in software design, teacher education and the use of computing environments in classrooms. Some of the examples we use are packages which have been available for some time; a few of them might be seen as really quite 'old'. We do not apologize for this. The examples we have chosen have been, and are being, widely used, and it is from the use and discussion of these that the ideas in the book have been developed.

This is not to say that the ideas are dated with the software with which they grew. On the contrary, the range in age of examples used throughout the text, from very old to very recent, supports our argument that the approach we advocate is not tied to a particular stage of development of the technology.

The book is structured in the following way. Some issues in, and early approaches to, the discussion and selection of educational software are considered in Chapter 2. Chapters 3, 4, and 5 look in some detail at checklists for assessing educational software, surveying available checklists, and critically examining this approach to software assessment.

Chapter 6 describes and analyzes frameworks and paradigms that have been developed to assist in the description and discussion of educational software. Then in Chapter 7 we introduce a paradigm that we will argue is more useful in the context of contemporary developments in software design and use. This paradigm uses the perspectives of the student, the teacher and the designer, and interactions between pairs of these perspectives to ensure a comprehensive view of educational software, and to assist in discussion of software selection and use. A major aim here is to enable greater emphasis to be placed on the intended use of a package when software selection decisions are being made.

The remainder of the book considers many of the issues of software assessment and use in a discussion structured by the paradigm. Chapter 8 looks at issues arising in the area of interaction of the perspectives of the student and the teacher. These concern the learning environment of the whole classroom, particularly learning activities sponsored by the software but occurring away from the computer itself. Increased student autonomy in learning, roles for teachers implied by this, and classroom interaction issues for software selection are considered.

In Chapter 9 issues arising in the area of interaction of the perspectives of the student and the designer are considered. The context for this chapter is provided by an outline of theories of learning. This leads to an examination of the issue of student control of learning activities in the computer environment. This is followed by discussion of levels of student control of educational software, complexity in learning environments, and the challenge implicit in software.

Chapter 10 looks at issues arising in the area of interaction of the perspectives of the designer and the teacher. Of particular interest in this context are issues of curriculum relevance, notably concerns with curriculum content and the processes supported by the use of educational software.

Chapter 11 concludes the book. The essential arguments are reviewed, and the validity of the new paradigm is examined in the light of likely future developments in educational software. The chapter ends with an exploration of the potential of the paradigm beyond software selection, including its value for evaluation, design and critical appraisal of the use of computers in education.

2 Selecting Educational Software

This chapter considers some issues in the selection of educational software. It looks at the quantity of software available for schools, opinions about the quality of these materials, and the need for teachers to develop skills in software selection. It considers similarities and differences between software selection and the selection of other classroom materials, and looks at some practical concerns in software selection. Sources of educational software are mentioned, and some ways in which teachers might find out about available software and keep up to date with this information are outlined.

At the end of the chapter some early work on criteria for use in software selection is outlined. This leads to consideration of the development of software assessment checklists to assist teachers in selection tasks; these are examined at some length in the next chapters.

Availability and Variety of Software for Education

For a time there was widespread dissatisfaction with the amount of software available for schools. This was expressed in a variety of quarters by teachers, educational advisers, conference speakers and writers in journals and magazines (see for example commentaries by Johnston, 1987; Preece and Jones, 1985). More recently the situation has changed somewhat, and schools now receive a steady stream of marketing materials from distributors and developers of educational software. A 1988 report estimated that more than 10,000 educational software products were then on the market in the USA (OTA, 1988), and between 1,000 and 4,000 in each country were estimated to exist in Australia, Canada, France, Italy and the UK in 1989 (OECD, 1989).

However, despite the increase in quantity, the quality of these products still varies widely. Many of the earliest programs contain real technical faults, although the packages may be nicely presented and, possibly, quite expensive.

Templeton describes some examples.

Here are a few of the kinds of nasties for which good money is being charged:

1 A program that tests your capacity for finding anagrams, that refuses to accept a perfectly good word.
2 A program that tests punctuation, that won't accept a valid alternative sentence.
3 An addition program that won't allow you to fill in the tens column before the units.
4 A disk-based program for which the only documentation available is for a cassette version with quite different facilities.
5 A program supposedly written by a teacher and intended for use by children which is literally full of spelling mistakes.
6 An information retrieval program that forces me to look over 100 consecutive records (or turn the machine off!)
7 A program that begins with the question:
   WHAT IS YOUR NAME? (NO MORE THAN SIX LETTERS)
8 A mathematics program for young children that contains several 'facts' that are mathematically quite erroneous.

(Templeton, 1985 p. 57).

As well as noting packages with such obvious technical faults, Templeton argues that some packages are also educationally unsound. He states that much educational software is actually setting the cause of good educational practice back by many years.

More recently technical quality has improved. A report from the USA Office of Technology Assessment (OTA) states that

The technical quality of most commercially produced software is quite good. However, there is a general consensus that most software does not yet sufficiently exploit the capacity of the computer to enhance teaching and learning. (OTA, 1988 p. 122)

Sound technical design does not guarantee educational value for a software package.

The vast majority of titles aim at basic skills. Software to teach 'higher order' skills, such as hypothesis testing and problem solving, is in much shorter supply. Drill and practice software continues to dominate all subject areas, to the chagrin of many educators and educational technologists. (OTA, 1988 p. 122)

Komoski, from the Educational Products Information Exchange (EPIE), a software reviewing agency in the USA, writes

Only about 7 per cent of the one thousand or so programs evaluated from 1982 through 1985 by EPIE's team of trained evaluators . . . have been judged to be of high enough overall quality to be designated 'highly recommended' for school and/ or home use. Only another 36 per cent have been judged good enough to be designated 'recommended with reservations'. The remaining 57 per cent . . . have been designated either 'not re-commended but may meet some needs' or 'do not consider'. (Komoski, 1987 p. 400)

However an OECD (1989) report cites Komoski as estimating that the proportion of good quality software among newly developed programs is increasing with time, and he goes on to state that

. . . despite the depressingly poor quality of so many programs, the qualitative side of educational software is not entirely bleak . . . the best of today's software may be capable of raising the standards — and expectations — for educational materials in general. . . . The best of today's software is extending the pedagogical range, capability and effectiveness of mediated learning in ways that no other medium has ever been able to do. (Komoski, 1987 p. 401)

Komoski argues that good use of graphics and text can provide teachers and learners with unprecedented flexibility and control, and that the best software can extend the range, depth and appropriateness of teaching and learning options beyond those traditionally available in classrooms. These can range from well-designed tutorials and highly motivating practice exercises, through simulations that can provide challenging true-to-life problems to learners, or problem solving software involving strategies beyond any of the problem solving techniques currently taught in today's textbooks, to software enabling students to search data bases containing a wide variety of curriculum-relevant information.

As the quantity of software available is increasing, so is the variety. This applies not only to technical quality, but also to the student learning styles (OECD, 1989) and classroom teaching approaches (Shingles, 1988) which software might support. With increasing chances of finding and using software that can provide valuable enhancement to learning in many situations, the task of selecting suitable packages for a particular class or educational purpose is becoming considerably more complex. Nevertheless, teachers need to be as adept at choosing software suitable for their purposes as they are at selecting textbooks, videotapes and other educational materials.

Software Review

Reviews of educational software are now common in professional educational and computing publications. However, there are some problems with review as a form of assessment. A fundamental problem arises from the use of a non-interactive medium, paper-based text, to report on the interactive medium of computer software. It is very difficult, if not impossible, to convey in the written word the essential aspects of a computer program, so software review is difficult, and possibly in a strict sense fundamentally inappropriate. The accuracy of reviews is also open to question:

> Many magazines devote considerable space to software reviews. These are usually written by computer-using teachers or by specialists in particular subject areas. But magazines are reluctant to publish negative reviews, in part for fear of alienating potential advertisers. (OTA, 1988 p. 135)

However experience has shown that reviews can be very useful, as evidenced by the growth of independent product review agencies.

> The booming educational software industry has led to the creation of independent product review organizations. Many of these are private, non-profit agencies supported by states, universities or school districts, individually or in consortia. These use a wide range of evaluation criteria and methodologies, and serve a diverse clientele. (OTA, 1988 p. 135)

Langhorne, Donham, Gross and Rehmke (1989) argue that reviews do not eliminate the need for previewing software, but that they are helpful in determining what to preview. This point of view is emphasized by Johnston:

> The ever increasing availability of commercially produced programs increases the need for such evaluative reviews, to disseminate information and assist in the process of selecting suitable course materials. (Johnston, 1987 p. 41)

Essentially review is a version of selection, in which software selection advice is given with a diverse audience in mind. Reading reviews can be a first step in the selection process, a way of finding out what is available for selection.

Who Should Choose Educational Software?

Not all teachers undertake selection of software, but strong arguments can be made for having the teachers who will use the software extensively involved in its selection (see for example Winship, 1988).

Software selection is carried out for various purposes. A computing co-ordinator or software librarian might be required to choose packages for inclusion in a school's software library, while a specific subject teacher will more often be involved in selecting software to supplement teaching in a particular subject. In the former case the criteria used for selection will probably put more emphasis on the attributes of a package itself than on the ways in which it might be used in class, as the selection is being carried out on behalf of others; the computing co-ordinator or librarian will probably not be the one to use the package with students. In the latter case the criteria for selection can put more emphasis on consideration of the classroom environment in which the software will be used, the abilities and interests of the students, preferred teaching methods, detailed curriculum considerations, and so on.

It is not necessarily a good idea, for example, for a computing teacher to choose on technical grounds a word processor to be used throughout a school. Rather, if a standard one is to be used (and there is a strong case in favour of adopting standards in this situation), teachers from all subject areas and levels who might use the package should try out available choices and be involved in the selection decisions.

Heller (1991) cites examples where software 'evaluation' has been carried out by students, by teachers, by administrators and by librarians. However, this writer states that classroom teachers

. . . are thought by most to be the most appropriate software reviewers. They know the day-to-day informational and ped-agogical needs of the students as well as curricular needs. (Heller, 1991 p. 286)

Langhorne *et al.* (1989) advocate a team-based approach to evaluation and decision-making.

Advantages to this approach are that it allows for maximizing the use of human resources while minimizing duplication of effort and inappropriate purchases. The varying instructional needs, teaching styles, and building philosophy brought to the evaluation process by each of the evaluators will lead to a much sounder decision than is likely to result from a single evalu-ation. (Langhorne *et al.*, 1989 p. 33)

These writers suggest that a team should include teachers, for content area knowledge and understanding of instructional strategies for spe-cific purposes, library and media specialists with experience in selec-tion of materials, and administrators who are familiar with computer-assisted learning and possess a working knowledge of instructional design.

Newman (1988) argues the need for a school software library, discussing the issues involved in establishing such a library and the types of software required. He suggests that catalogues and other infor-mation from and about sources of software come to the software librar-ian, whose task it is to encourage appropriate staff members to preview particular packages and recommend purchase or otherwise.

Software Browsing

Teachers are both competent and confident at browsing through books, kits, videotapes and other materials to select resources which will support and assist their endeavours, and generally they have the opportunity to review such materials before they purchase them. However, this has not been the case with software. The fact that educational software containing faults such as those listed earlier in this chapter is sold at all has been partly a result of limited opportunities for teachers to browse through software before purchasing. More recently such opportunit-ies are being made available through review copy arrangements or provisions for demonstrations and browsing by some distributors, as well as through teachers' centres, in-service courses, and displays at conferences. Fortunately, the expectation that software purchase decisions can be made based only on information from sales brochures and word of mouth is disappearing.

Many of the skills needed for browsing through software are similar to those used by teachers selecting other classroom resources, but there are significant differences as well, as indicated by Johnston.

> The evaluation of microcomputer programs is unlike that of learning materials in other educational media in general, and of the book in particular, in that software is not readily accessible to inspection by skimming, scanning and the selection of random parts for detailed examination. . . . The only way to determine a program's suitability for a particular educational purpose and teaching style is to run it and explore it thoroughly. (Johnston, 1987 p. 45).

In the next section we shall look at various sources of software for schools since the source of a software package can, in the first instance, give some indication about its likely style and character.

Sources of Software for Schools

Software for school use is distributed by several different types of organizations. Some major publishers of books and other educational materials now publish software as well. Successful book publishing does not necessarily imply expertise in software publishing, but such companies usually produce a professional product. The packages are often marketed by a separate division of the publishing company.

More recently publishers specializing in microcomputer software have appeared, and these are anxious to develop and maintain good reputations for quality software and customer support. Their products are generally available from computer shops or from specialist software distributors.

Publicly funded educational organizations and curriculum development projects also produce software for school use. These groups should be relatively free from the commercial constraints and pressures that exist for regular publishers, so they have the potential to produce more innovative or adventurous materials. Often their software can be made available at subsidized cost. Publicity for these packages may be circulated within a limited group so it can be difficult to find out about or to obtain them.

Computer clubs and the user groups associated with particular makes of computers provide facilities, with various degrees of formality, for sharing and trading of software. At the most informal level this involves members taking disks to meetings, to exchange programs they have written for those written by others. There are wider, more formally run user groups associated with specific types of computer, and these have newsletters or other publications in which members are invited to submit their programs for inclusion in a catalogue of user-written materials for wider distribution. Public domain and 'shareware' products are accessible through electronic bulletin boards, interest groups and various cooperative organizations. These are typically produced by teachers, students and computer buffs to fill specific curriculum niches that commercial developers have neglected (OTA, 1988). Programs obtained through these organizations are generally less expensive than those described earlier, but they may be less professionally produced, perhaps lacking extensive testing, documentation or arrangements for maintenance and user support.

It is not possible to present here an exhaustive and current list of sources of educational software. However, these examples should provide an overview of the nature and range of sources of educational software, and give some feeling for the types of materials which are available.

Finding Out What is Available

Many of the companies and other sources mentioned send software catalogues and other advertising materials directly to schools, usually addressed either to the headteacher or principal, or the co-ordinator of computing. Teachers from other areas in the school may need to ask these staff members to pass on to them information about software related to their particular subject areas or interests. Individual teachers can also arrange to be included on the mailing lists of publishers whose materials are of relevance to them.

There are a number of educational computing magazines and journals, distinct from computer hobbyist magazines. These publications often contain reviews of recently released materials as well as advertisements for software distributors and products. School and local librarians, other teachers, advisory teachers or staff in teacher training institutions can suggest and recommend titles of these publications. In fact these people can themselves be valuable sources of information about available software and related materials.

Teacher and professional organizations, not only in computing but in other subject areas as well, publish newsletters and journals in which computing resources are reviewed and discussed. Many of these organizations run conferences and in-service education activities at which computer use in appropriate contexts is considered, and relevant software is examined. At larger conferences, particularly those focusing on educational computing themes, there are often exhibition areas where materials from software producers and distributors are displayed.

Most education departments and authorities have now established centres which maintain extensive libraries of software, with machines and assistance available, for teachers to visit and browse. These centres usually display a range of books and printed materials about educational computing as well.

Teachers might write directly to larger educational computing or software development projects which can provide catalogues of other information about software. And, of course, visits to local computer shops and dealerships to examine software products can be most worthwhile.

A number of software clearing houses or agencies have been set up by education authorities or independent non-profit bodies in order to review educational software (Heller, 1991; OECD, 1989). Many of these maintain information databases in print or electronic media to provide information to help teachers select software.

Some Criteria for Software Selection

It was recognized very early in the development of educational computing that there was a need to develop practical criteria to help teachers to assess educational software. Work done on the development of these criteria has helped in the formulation of later approaches, so we will now examine some statements of these criteria.

There is now quite an extensive literature on the subject of software selection. (As mentioned earlier, the word 'evaluation' has also been used often in this sense). Many among the earlier publications outlined criteria to apply or questions to ask about the attributes of a software package. These questions generally fell into two groups.

The first group consisted of general criteria, essentially the same as those which teachers were thought to use already in the assessment of other classroom materials. We shall use the list suggested by Rawitsch (1983) to illustrate typical questions in this group.

1　Is the subject matter covered accurately?
2　Is the material written at an appropriate reading level?
3　Are the activities of appropriate length?
4　Are clear, concise instructions given for students?
5　Are the activities sequenced logically?
6　Is the layout of the materials appealing?
7　Is correct grammar used in the materials?
8　Are the activities motivating for the students?
9　Are the materials socially acceptable?
10　Are the support materials complete?
11　Is the cost reasonable for the value received?

(Rawitsch, 1983 p. 346)

The second group of criteria was more specifically related to the use of computers and computing as an educational resource. These questions were generally more technical. Again we will use Rawitsch's list as an example.

1　Is the interactive capability of the computer used to advantage?
2　Are special capabilities, such as the ability to produce random events, used to advantage?
3　Are features such as graphics, animation, and sound used in ways that enhance instruction as opposed to simply making the presentation more 'flashy'?
4　Does the software allow the teacher and students appropriate control over the activity by providing options for movement through the materials?
5　Does the computer handle input from the student effectively, so that excessive typing is avoided and unexpected student responses do not disrupt the activity?
6　Is reinforcement for correct and incorrect student responses and performance provided effectively and appropriately?

(Rawitsch, 1983 pp. 346–7)

As well in this second group were questions concerning the style and structure of the package, illustrated by the following list from Preece and Squires (1984).

1　Does the program produce realistic and valid results?
2　Is the program easy to operate?
3　Is the program versatile to use?

4   Is the program attractive and motivating?
5   Is the software robust?
6   Is the package well documented?

(Preece and Squires, 1984 p. 20)

Clearly these lists are not exhaustive, and people choosing software for different schools, subject areas, age levels and so on would regard different attributes as more important. However, the criteria suggested in publications like these did provide some guidelines for teachers making software selection decisions.

Software evaluation forms and checklists incorporating sets of questions about attributes of software packages were a natural outcome of the early identification of selection criteria such as those cited. Checklists have been used widely in software selection and review, giving a structure to these tasks. These are examined at some length in Chapters 3, 4, and 5.

3   Checklists for Software Assessment

Chapters 3, 4, and 5 focus on the checklist approach to selection of educational software. Checklists have been used extensively for software selection, in every country where educational software is used. In fact we have not been able to find any other systematic method for software selection in use at all. In support of this, an article on software selection and review titled 'Evaluating Software: A Review of the Options' (Heller, 1991) surveys a large range of assessment forms and checklists developed in the USA; no options other than these are mentioned.

Many lists of criteria for assessment of individual packages have been developed. Some have been produced at the individual or school level, and others by larger organizations. They vary in content, length and style, but all have been designed in an attempt to help teachers choose software of educational value. We shall look in this chapter at a number of these, to illustrate their differences and similarities, and to enable a relatively thorough study of this major approach to software selection. Several influential or interesting checklists are described, in some cases briefly, in the body of the chapter, and the full checklists are shown in chronological order in a series of Appendixes at the end of the book. A table summarizing these and other available checklists of which we are aware, is included. The chapter concludes with a short comparative analysis of the checklists presented.

Three Representative Checklists

Three checklists which are representative of common checklist designs are described in this section.

MicroSIFT Evaluator's Guide (1982)

First we shall look at an American example, an *Evaluator's Guide for Microcomputer-Based Instructional Packages*, developed by the software reviewing agency, Microcomputer Software Information for Teachers (MicroSIFT). MicroSIFT was the first clearing house for information about educational software. It was established in 1979 with federal funding, at the Northwest Regional Educational Laboratory in Oregon, USA (OECD, 1989).

A major activity for the agency was the design and development of an instrument on which to base the review process. The resulting checklist is included in a booklet which explains fully the meaning of each criterion, and provides some sample reviews. The criteria are grouped into those concerning the content of the package, those concerning instructional quality, and those concerning technical quality. The full checklist is shown in Appendix A. The booklet is titled *Evaluator's Guide*, but the word is used here to refer as well to the processes we are calling review and selection. This is clear from the introduction to the booklet, which states that it is designed to be '. . . a tool for writing carefully documented, thorough software reviews'. (MicroSIFT, 1982 p. 6). For in-service and pre-service education students and for practitioners it aims to provide '. . . a structured format for evaluating and selecting courseware . . . It has been found useful by individual teachers or others wishing to evaluate courseware before purchasing'. (MicroSIFT, 1982 pp. 6–7) The checklist developers suggest that '. . . the *Evaluator's Guide* gives people who are writing or revising software a checklist to judge the instructional worth of their courseware'. (MicroSIFT, 1982 p. 6)

However, they see its role less in formative evaluation than in selection, as '. . . it is not expected that student use of a package be observed in this evaluation process. You, as a professional, are making a judgement based on your teaching experience in the grade level and subjects intended for the package'. (MicroSIFT, 1982 p. 15)

Software Evaluation (Salvas and Thomas, 1984)

Next we shall consider a checklist developed in Australia by Salvas and Thomas (1984) for the Education Department of Victoria. This form has been widely distributed and used in that state. It was published as part of a fourteen-page booklet on software 'evaluation', although again the intent is that the list be used for selection and review.

The developers of this checklist emphasize that they do not claim to provide a definitive classification system for good and bad software; rather they attempt to offer guidelines for teachers on how to select suitable software, highlighting commonly occurring problems and drawing attention to factors which can easily be overlooked.

The booklet describes eight types of educational programs: information retrieval, drill and practise, games, modelling, simulation, tutorial, applications packages such as word processors and spreadsheets, and teaching support programs. Then, after discussing what is meant by each type, the authors present a list of questions to be considered in assessing a package. The questions are broadly grouped into some which could be answered by referring to the documentation of the program, and others concerning the program itself. The latter group is divided into Teacher Evaluation Criteria and Student Evaluation Criteria. Each of these subsections begins with questions labelled Educational Criteria, followed by groups of questions for Functional Criteria, Machine Exploitation, Supplementary Materials, and, for the Teacher section, groups of questions on User Reactions and Screen Criteria. The full questionnaire is shown in Appendix B.

Choosing Educational Software (Blease, 1986)

Typically, the literature on evaluation of educational software takes the form of journal articles, conference papers, evaluation booklets and reports. Blease, working in the United Kingdom, has published a more extended treatment in a book *Evaluating Educational Software* (Blease, 1986). Our next example is from this work.

Blease does distinguish separate meanings for software selection and evaluation, suggesting that these are two stages of the process of differentiating between potentially good software and the rest. His treatment of software selection is in a chapter entitled 'Choosing Educational Software', intended to be '. . . a detailed examination of software selection and what to look out for when choosing programs for classroom use. It is aimed at those who have to make a choice without being able to try the software with children in the classroom'. (Blease, 1986 p. 12)

Blease has assembled a set of questions by taking the most commonly occurring criteria from some of the 'already numerous examples available in the literature' (Blease, 1986 p. 73). He groups the questions under five headings: Documentation, Presentation and Layout, Friendliness and Flexibility, Achievement of Stated Aims, and Robustness. He explains what is meant by each criterion, often using specific examples, and refers to all of these as General Selection Criteria.

He lists separately groups of criteria which pertain more specifically to particular types of packages: tutorial programs, drill and practice, arcade-type games, simulation games, laboratory simulations, and content-free tools such as data-bases. He does this to avoid what he regards as a major weakness in checklists, that they almost always contain selection criteria which are inappropriate to the program being studied. Blease's lists are given in full in Appendix H.

Further Examples of Checklists

Guidelines for Educational Software Selection (Coburn et al., 1985)

Coburn, Kelman, Roberts, Snyder, Watt and Weiner (1985), in their book *Practical Guide to Computers in Education*, include a set of guidelines for educational software selection. These are in the form of sets of questions grouped under headings, Program Content, Pedagogy, Program Operation, and Student Outcomes. Each question is explained and discussed at length, and the writers provide examples to illustrate the issues raised. A list of the question groups is provided in Appendix D. This book, from the USA, has been widely used in teacher training courses, and its advice on software selection must be seen as influential.

Software Selection Criteria (Preece and Jones, 1985)

The next example is a British checklist also designed specifically for teacher education. Preece and Jones (1985) used a 'selection criteria sheet' developed for the purpose as part of an Open University course to enhance teachers' skills in software selection. This sheet presents a series of criteria under headings Educational Documentation, Achievement of Stated Aims, Appropriateness of the Micro and Program, Screen Presentation, Friendliness and Flexibility of the Program, Technical Documentation, and Summary of Overall Impressions, inviting the teacher to give the program a score from 1 to 5 (or Not Applicable) for each. The complete list of criteria is shown in Appendix E.

Choosing Software (Templeton, 1985)

In a contribution to a book for parents on educational software, Templeton (1985) discusses the use of educational software in the home. He warns parents of some of the problems of finding good programs, and provides a list of points to consider before purchase. These are grouped into Basic Considerations, concerning the hardware needed, the reputation of the publisher, and so on; Educational Considerations, some questions to help non-teachers; and Special Considerations, suitable use of a computer, flexibility of the program, learner motivation and control of activities, and so on. We have included this list as it is the only one we have found directed particularly at parent purchasers of software. The complete list is included as Appendix G.

Guidelines for Software in Reading (Krause, 1984)

Miller and Burnett (1986), in a paper on selection of software for language teaching, discuss a set of guidelines for choosing software for teaching reading developed by Krause (1984). Miller and Burnett indicate that Krause's guidelines are quite typical of those found in articles on software evaluation for language development. We have included it as an example of a checklist designed for selection of software in a specific subject area. A condensed version of the guidelines, as provided in the article by Miller and Burnett, is shown in Appendix C.

Evaluating Software for the Classrooom (Reay, 1985)

Reay sees a need for '. . . an approach to evaluating software which is general enough to be widely applicable but specific enough to provide the kind of information that will allow decisions to be made about the acceptability of programs under consideration' (Reay, 1985 p. 80).

Reay worked with teachers in the USA and England for three years to develop a checklist designed for teachers, or groups of teachers involved in the selection of software. This checklist is particularly interesting as it implies two ways of classifying software: by program type (drill and practice, tutorials, simulations, and so on) and by concern with types of learning (concept learning, rule learning, memory training, problem-solving and practice). The checklist is shown in Appendix F.

Evaluating Educational Software (OTA, 1988)

The USA Office of Technology Assessment was asked to prepare a report to assist the House Committee on Education and Labor 'to better understand the potential of new interactive technologies for improving learning' (OTA, 1988 p. iii). As part of this substantial project many issues related to educational software were studied. The researchers found that among the thirty-six public, private and governmental software review organizations surveyed '. . . there is considerable overlap in the definition of quality criteria. A complete list of the criteria includes more than 200 items, the majority of which pertain to technical characteristics rather than learning effects' (OTA, 1988 p. 136).

Based on items used by the software evaluation agencies, and additional items from 'selected teachers, software publishers, university professors, and private consultants' (OTA, 1988 p. 232), the project assembled a large list of characteristics considered in assessing educational software. These are grouped under main headings, Instructional Quality, Teacher Modifiability, Evaluation and Recordkeeping, Documentation and Support Materials, Technical Quality, and Hardware and Marketing Issues, with further sub-grouping under each heading. The complete list is shown in Appendix I.

Questions to Ask Before Purchasing CD-ROM (NCET, 1992)

The British National Council for Educational Technology (NCET) carried out a study to evaluate the potential of CD-ROM software for classroom use. An Appendix to the evaluation report (NCET, 1992b) lists a set of 'questions to ask before purchasing CD-ROM', and we include this list as it is very recent at the time of writing, and because it is designed for the new technology of CD-ROM. The list of questions is shown in Appendix J.

Summary of Checklists

Table 3.1 summarizes the checklists we have encountered in our reading in this area. It is not an exhaustive list, but should give readers some idea of the work done on the development of checklists for software assessment. Complete citations for all of the checklists are given in the Bibliography.

In the USA further checklists have been developed by software

Table 3.1   Summary of Checklists

Source/Author	Year	Title
Heck, Johnson and Kansky	1981	*Guidelines for Evaluating Computerized Instructional Materials* (cited in Johnston, 1987)
MicroSIFT	1982	*Evaluator's Guide for Microcomputer-Based Instructional Packages*
Salvas and Thomas	1982	*Evaluation of Software,* Education Department of Victoria, Australia
Krause	1984	*Choosing Computer Software That Works* (cited in Miller and Burnett, 1986)
Burt	1985	*Software in the Classroom — A Form for Teacher Use* (cited in Heller, 1991)
Coburn *et al.*	1985	*Guidelines for Educational Software Selection*
Ministers of Education, Canada	1985	*Software Evaluation* (cited in Smith and Keep, 1988)
Preece and Jones	1985	*Software Selection Criteria*
Reay	1985	*Evaluating Software for the Classroom*
Templeton	1985	*Choosing Software*
Blease	1986	*Choosing Educational Software: General Selection Criteria, Specific Selection Criteria*
Schall, Leake and Whitaker	1986	*Computer Education* (cited in Heller, 1991)
Office of Technology Assessment	1988	*Characteristics Considered in Evaluating Educational Software*
EDUCOM	1989	*Software Snapshots: Where Are You in the Picture?* (cited in Heller, 1991)
National Council for Educational Technology	1992	*Some Questions To Ask Before Purchasing CD-ROM*

review agencies including the Educational Products Information Exchange (EPIE), Minnesota Educational Computing Consortium (MECC), the National Council of Teachers of English, and the National Council of Teachers of Mathematics, as well as by many independent groups (Heller, 1991).

It is not possible, and would not assist our overall argument, to provide a comprehensive list of all the checklists that have been developed for the assessment of educational software. However, the examples described, and the full listings in the Appendixes, should give the reader a good idea of the nature and range of these assessment instruments.

Almost all of the checklists contain a considerable number of items concerning the hardware needed to run the program, the presence and quality of documentation and printed support materials, the topic area and content of the program, its ease of use and reliability of operation, and the use of colour, graphics and sound in the program. Most group these items under headings, although there is considerable variation in the way this organization is done and in the headings used, depending to some extent on the country of origin of the list, its specific purpose, and, no doubt, on the preferences of particular checklist designers.

Many also include items classified as educational or instructional criteria, concerning learning objectives, topic relevance to curriculum, student control over pace and stopping the program, quality of feedback to the learner, motivation characteristics of the program, and its capabilities for assessing and keeping records of student performance.

The huge range of items and item types used in checklist design is revealed by the size of the list resulting from the OTA (1988) survey of 'Characteristics Considered in Evaluating Educational Software' (Appendix I). Some of the checklists encourage further unstructured comments from the assessor.

It would seem then that the assessment of educational software by means of checklists should by now be a well-developed, effective and much appreciated technique. In fact this is not the case. As we have noted the checklist approach is indeed widely advocated, but it is also the subject of a good deal of criticism. Its wide advocacy is, perhaps, more a result of there being no real alternative than because it is an entirely satisfactory technique for guiding the process of software selection. In the next chapter we shall begin an examination of the effectiveness of the checklist approach to the assessment of educational software.

4   Examination of the Checklist Approach in Software Selection

We shall argue, later, that the checklist approach to selection of educational software has significant limitations, and we begin our case in this chapter. First we shall look at an experiment conducted by Blease (1986) to 'test' the validity of one particular checklist, that developed by Preece and Jones (1985). Then we shall consider several actual software packages, and examine carefully the extent to which some of the checklists presented in Chapter 3 enable us to express a clear and useful assessment of the programs, such as would be of value in making selection decisions.

Investigating the Validity of One Checklist

Blease (1986) describes an experiment carried out to investigate the validity of checklists in general, and in particular the checklist devised by Preece and Jones (1985) described in the previous chapter. In the same year as Preece and Jones carried out the evaluation of the teacher education course for which their checklist was developed, Blease taught a similar course, to a relatively similar group of students and using the same materials, at his university. In both courses each student's scores on the individual checklist criteria were combined to make single summary ratings, and these were compared for the two groups of students. Blease describes the results of the experiment as follows.

> Although one might not expect the two groups of scores to agree exactly, it might be reasonable to expect that the pattern of scores might be similar as one goes down the lists. If they were, we might be able to say that, although the numerical scores themselves are of little meaning, the check-list itself appears to be fairly consistent when it is used by different groups

of teachers looking at the same programs. If this were the case then it would suggest that perhaps other people's assessment could function as a reliable guide for those who read them. Now of course we must accept that the sample size in this experiment is small, and that the two courses, though very similar, were not the same. However, a simple non-parametric test of correlation, (the Pearson Product Moment Correlation Coefficient), between the average summary ratings of the two exercises, for both programs, revealed absolutely no statistically significant association between the two sets of ratings whatsoever. This would seem to further suggest that the numerical scores are quite arbitrary, being subject to the individual teacher's past experience and very personal ideas about what could be done using that program with a particular class. . . . What was particularly interesting, however, was the striking similarity between the written comments about the two programs made by the two groups of teachers. (Blease, 1986 p. 71)

Blease did find significant differences for one of the programs, between the scores of one group which contained teachers who had previously used that program in the classroom and the other group in which none had classroom experience of the program. 'It just happens that "Pirates" is a program which performs better in the classroom, than one might expect from just looking at its rather unimaginative screen display' (Blease, 1986 p. 71).

The main conclusions reached by Blease as a result of this study are as follows.

1   Beware of numerical and star ratings, they are not as objective as they may appear.
2   Written or verbal descriptions and comments are probably more reliable as a general guide.
3   Remember that your selection, and that of others, depends on what you, or they intend doing with the program. The decisions you make about its suitability or 'worth' depend a great deal on your past experience, not just as a computer user, but as a teacher as well. You must also bear this in mind when you read other people's assessment, especially if you do not know who they are and how they work.

(Blease, 1986 p. 72)

We want to investigate further the issue of the use of checklists for software selection. The method we shall use is different from that of

Blease; we shall use several checklists, and simply examine the extent to which we are able to express with them what we want to say about particular programs. Our 'experiment' begins in the next section.

Examination of the Checklist Approach: *The Flowers of Crystal* Package

We shall take as our first example a well-known software package, an adventure game called *Flowers of Crystal* (Matson, 1984) written for primary school children. This program has become somewhat of a software 'classic' as, despite its age, it is still widely used in schools. The original version was written for the BBC microcomputer, the program was re-written for the Apple II, and most recently an Apple Macintosh version has been completed. The package is 'used very successfully in a number of countries' (OECD, 1989 p. 43).

The *Flowers of Crystal* package consists of a software disk, a booklet of teachers' notes, an illustrated story booklet, an audio-cassette of the story, a tourist map of the planet Crystal, and several student worksheets for keeping records of work done with the program. The package was written to provide the basis for a lengthy project, and its aim is stated in the opening words of the teachers' notes: '*Flowers of Crystal* was designed to provide a stimulus for creative activities within the classroom' (Matson, 1984 p. 5).

The teachers' booklet includes some user notes on the programs in the package, a section on using the package in the classroom, suggested paths through the program, some comments, project ideas and suggestions for work cards from teachers who have used the program in class, and a list of resources which might be used for related project work.

The program is based on a story about the imaginary planet Crystal. Over-development for tourism has ravaged the once beautiful planet. The bubble gum factory of the profit-hungry Mr. Grubble provides bubble gum for the horrible Blids who live underground on Crystal. By coming to the surface to get the gum, the Blids risked being killed by the Crystal Flowers. Mr. Grubble, to protect his commercial interests, has killed all the Crystal Flowers and none now remain on the planet. Underground tunnelling by the increased population of Blids has caused the collapse of many buildings, but although the Crystallians protest, Mr. Grubble has hired tough bodyguards to protect him and do his work. No tourists come to Crystal now, and most Crystallians are becoming very poor.

In earlier days on Crystal an old woman, Rumala, anticipating the troubles, prepared a plan for the survival of the planet. She collected items such as special soil, water and fertiliser, and hid them in various secret places on the planet, protecting them with magic spells. Then she hid one Crystal Flower plant, surrounding it also with magic.

A special Crystallian, Jim, has seen in the sky messages from Rumala about the hidden Flower, but he must have the assistance of people from another world to find it. And so the task of the students, the 'visitors' to Crystal from planet Earth, is to find the hidden articles and the last Flower of Crystal.

The role of the package as a stimulus for much off-computer activity is emphasized by what is *not* provided in the program. Matson writes in the teacher's handbook:

> Many of the scenes and characters in the programs (and in . . . [the] illustrations) are deliberately vague. The intention is to stimulate the imagination. If a Blid is never seen it will exist in numerous forms in the classroom. Likewise there are many unanswered questions in the adventure. Why is it never possible to get to the mountains? What exactly are Zap Gates and who put them there? What do the spells look like and how can they have different properties? Who or what are the Exiles? Part 2 ends quite abruptly when the Crystal Flower is located. Perhaps the story is only just beginning at this point. How is the flower to be used? Is Crystal saved? What happens to Grubble? Do the visitors from Earth return home? (Matson, 1984 p. 9)

The ideas for project work suggested in the teacher's booklet include many activities in diverse curriculum areas: language development, mathematics, science, history, geography, art, drama and music. The package is quite widely used in primary schools, often as the thematic focus for a major unit of work across curriculum areas as suggested.

A videotape, *Flowers for the Teacher*, has been made showing the activities that one class undertook in a six week unit of work based on the program. The children made posters and advertising materials for Grubble's bubble gum, and then did a marketing presentation for critical class members to taste new flavours of gum and assess their sales potential. They interviewed a student, playing the role of Mr. Grubble, about his company, his income, his motives, the sources of his workers and some ecological issues. Another role play involved a debate between Crystallian conservationists and developers, on questions concerning ecology and quality of life. Drama and movement activities included work with 'Grubble's grabbers' and with the Blids. The children further described and discussed the appearance and habits of the

SOFTWARE EVALUATION

Reviewer ....*Anne McDougall*.............   Date...........................

Name of Program.......*Flowers of Crystal* ....   Version.......................

Author .....*Mike Matson*......................................

Manufacturer/Distributor ......*4 MATION*...

Cost $

Subject/Course ......⎯⎯⎯...........................

Age/Year Level ......*Primary*.......................

Brand of Machine ....*BBC/Apple*........   Memory Required ..*32*.. K

Disc Drives Required (No.) ...*1*...   Printer   (Y /(N))

Application Type ..*Adventure Game*...

Teacher Notes   Poor 1 2 3 4 ⑤ Excellent

Student Notes   Poor 1 2 ③ 4 5 Excellent

Are sample results provided?   ((Y)/ N)

If so, rate them   Poor 1 2 3 4 ⑤ Excellent

Is the documentation easily understood?   ((Y)/ N)

TEACHER EVALUATION CRITERIA

Educational Criteria
Does the program:
(a)	fit my syllabus?	Y /(N)
(b)	have a clearly defined topic?	Y /(N)
(c)	match my educational philosophy?	(Y)/ N
(d)	use the same methodology for all students?	(Y)/ N
(e)	suit a variety of users?	(Y)/ N
(f)	suit the group I have in mind?	(Y)/ N
(g)	develop social skills?	(Y)/ N

(h) suit (please tick)
- (i)   individual use   [√]
- (ii)   small groups   [√]
- (iii)   large group   [√]
- (iv)   whole class   [√]

User Reaction
Does the program:
(a)	motivate the user?	(Y)/ N
(b)	allow student interaction?	(Y)/ N

Screen Criteria
(a)	Is the display easily read?	(Y)/ N
(b)	Is the language appropriate for my students?	(Y)/ N
(c)	Is the nature of the user input clearly indicated?	(Y)/ N

Functional Criteria
(a)	Is the program easy to start?	(Y)/ N
(b)	Are input errors easily corrected?	(Y)/ N
(c)	Does incorrect data entry cause termination of the program?	Y /(N)
(d)	Can students use the program independently?	(Y)/ N
(e)	Does the program access the disc during the program's operation?	(Y)/ N

Machine exploitation
(a)	Does the software make good use of the computer's features?	? Y / N

Supplementary Materials
(a)	Do the worksheets provide a useful follow-up to the program?	(Y)/ N
(b)	Does the program provide useful feedback to the teacher?	Y /(N)

STUDENT EVALUATION CRITERIA

Educational Criteria
(a) Is the structure of the program flexible for the user?   Y /Ⓝ
(b) Is diagnostic assistance part of the program?   Y /Ⓝ

Functional Criteria
(a) Are the instructions clear?   Ⓨ/ N
(b) Can the user recall the instructions?   Ⓨ/ N
(c) Can the user control rate of delivery and level of difficulty?   Ⓨ/ N

Machine Exploitation
(a) Are special effects wisely used?   Ⓨ/ N

Supplementary Materials
(a) Do the worksheets provide meaningful activities?   Ⓨ/ N

Your reactions to the program including further comments on any of the above questions.

....

....

....

....

Figure 4.1   Assessment of 'Flowers of Crystal' Using Education Department of Victoria Evaluation Proforma

Blids in painting, clay modelling and written work. The class examined and drew maps of Crystal and of more Earthly localities. They grew bean plants in containers under various conditions in the classroom and measured the growth of the plants. Language work associated with the program was extensive. Oral planning and discussion took place in groups before and during the groups' sessions at the computer. The children wrote up each of their 'missions' at the computer afterwards in detail in log books, a task which took up to two days each time. The class considered here had forty children and one computer. The children took turns, in groups of five, to work at the machine. However the major part of their work during the unit was away from the computer, writing, drawing, planning, debating, role-playing, and so on. The teacher, the children and their parents interviewed for the videotape were all enthusiastic about the value of the work done by the class during the unit based around the program. While the videotape interviews were clearly made to promote the package, these views on the value of the program are in fact more widely held. It is clearly a package which can sponsor and focus a wide variety of valuable classroom activities for primary school children.

Using Checklists to Assess 'Flowers of Crystal'

Figures 4.1, 4.2 and 4.3 show the results of our assessments of the *Flowers of Crystal* package using three of the checklists discussed

RATING: Circle the letter abbreviation which best reflects your judgment.
(Use the space following each item for comments.)
IMPORTANCE: Circle the letter which reflects your judgment of the relative importance of the item in this evaluation.
☑ Check this box if the evaluation is based partly on your observation of student use of this package.

PACKAGE TITLE _____
REVIEWER'S NAME _____
VERSION _____
DATE OF REVIEW _____

Northwest Regional Educational Laboratory

COURSEWARE EVALUATION

RATING
SA — Strongly agree
A — Agree
D — Disagree
SD — Strongly disagree
NA — Not Applicable

IMPORTANCE (optional)
H — Higher
L — Lower

Category	Item	Rating	Importance
CONTENT	1. The content is accurate. (p.15)	SA A D SD **(NA)**	H **(L)**
	2. The content has educational value. (p.15)	SA A D SD **(NA)**	**(H)** L
	3. The content is free of race, ethnic, sex, and other stereotypes. (p.16)	**(SA)** A D SD NA	**(H)** L
	4. The purpose of the package is well-defined. (p.16)	**(SA)** A D SD NA	**(H)** L
	5. The package achieves its defined purpose. (p.16) *Depends how it is used*	SA A D SD NA	**(H)** L
	6. Presentation of content is clear and logical. (p. 33) *But the content isn't what's learnt*	SA **(A)** D SD NA	**(H)** L
	7. The level of difficulty is appropriate for the target audience. (p. 33)	SA **(A)** D SD NA	**(H)** L
INSTRUCTIONAL QUALITY	8. Graphics/color/sound are used for appropriate instructional reasons. (p. 34)	**(SA)** A D SD NA	**(H)** L
	9. Use of the package is motivational. (p. 34)	**(SA)** **(A)** D SD NA	**(H)** L
	10. The package effectively stimulates student creativity. (p. 34) *Depends how it is used.*	SA A D SD NA	**(H)** L
	11. Feedback on student responses is effectively employed. (p. 35)	SA A D SD **(NA)**	**(H)** L
	12. The learner controls the rate and sequence of presentation and review. (p. 36)	SA A D SD **(NA)**	**(H)** L
	13. Instruction is integrated with previous student experience. (p. 36) *Depends how it is used*	SA A D SD NA	**(H)** L
	14. Learning is generalizable to an appropriate range of situations. (p. 36) ? ? ?	SA A D SD NA	**(H)** L

TECHNICAL QUALITY			
SA (A) D SD NA	(H)	L	15. The user support materials are comprehensive. (p. 37)
SA A D SD (NA) ?	(H)	L	16. The user support materials are effective. (p. 38) ? ?
SA (A) D SD NA	(H)	L	17. Information displays are effective. (p. 39)
SA (A) D SD NA	(H)	L	18. Intended users can easily and independently operate the program. (p. 40)
SA A D SD NA	(H)	L	19. Teachers can easily employ the package. (p. 41) ? ?
SA A D SD (NA)	H	(L)	20. The program appropriately uses relevant computer capabilities. (p. 42)
SA (A) D SD NA	(H)	L	21. The program is reliable in normal use. (p. 42)

22. (Check one only) (p. 43)
☒ I would use or recommend use of this package with little or no change.
  (Note suggestions for effective use under Section 25.)
☐ I would use or recommend use of this package only if certain changes were made.
  (Note recommended changes under Section 24.)
☐ I would not use or recommend this package. (Note reasons under Section 24.)

microSIFT

23. Describe the major strengths of the package. (p. 43)

Motivation. Stimulus for record keeping, discussion, group work, activities in a wide variety of curriculum areas.

24. Describe the major weaknesses of the package. (p. 44)

? ? Not relevant to curriculum topic ? ?

25. Describe the potential use of the package in classroom settings. (p. 44)

Longer project or theme work for class, including many off-computer activities in many curriculum areas.

Figure 4.2 Assessment of 'Flowers of Crystal' Using MicroSIFT Courseware Evaluation Form

earlier in Chapter 3. Readers may of course disagree on various points within these assessments.

The package rates well on its documentation and presentation aspects, and on the more technical questions. In the second and third checklists the questions on flexibility were difficult to answer. Although there are many possible routes through the program, students are constrained to choose from set alternatives, and the way in which they interact with the program is fixed. Further, although the program itself is not really flexible, one feels that the classroom environment it engenders could be very flexible. Similarly, the second checklist's questions on diagnostic assistance and feedback to the teacher were

CHOOSING EDUCATIONAL SOFTWARE: GENERAL SELECTION CRITERIA

Documentation

(i) Technical

Does the program have any accompanying documentation? *Yes*

Are there any simple loading and running instructions? *Yes*

Does the program require anything other than the most elementary knowledge of the computer to get it up and running? *No*

Are hardware requirements made explicit in the simplest of terms? *Yes*

Are instructions given for making a back-up copy of the tape or disc? If not, do the publishers offer a replacement service for corrupted discs and tapes? *?*

Does the documentation include a list of other machines for which a version of the program is available? *Yes*

(ii) Program information

Are the aims and objectives of the program made clear? *Yes*

Does it specify the age and ability range for which it was designed: What degree of flexibility does it provide? *?*

What kind of program is it? *Adventure Game*

Does the program allow for any alterations to be made? If so, are the instructions unambiguous and easy for the non-expert to follow? *No Alterations*

Does the documentation contain instructions for a 'browse mode' or details of a 'sample run'? *Yes*

Presentation and Layout

Are instructions clear and unambiguous? *Yes*

Is each frame attractively presented avoiding irrelevant detail? *Yes*

Have coloured and double height characters been used to their best advantage? *Yes*

Is the use of graphics appropriate to the aims and objectives of the program? *Yes*

If pictures and diagrams are included, could they be represented more effectively by some other means? e.g. a printed sheet, a map or a photograph. *?*

If sound effects are included, do they constitute an essential and integral part of the program? *?*

Does the program provide a simple means whereby the volume can be controlled or the sound can be turned off completely? *Yes*

Friendliness and Flexibility

Does the program provide helpful messages to correct errors? *N.A.*

Is sufficient help provided so that pupils can understand the program without your constant intervention? *Yes*

Is the program sufficiently versatile so that the user can control what it does? *Yes*

Is the program sufficiently flexible to be applicable in a variety of teaching/learning situations? *Yes*

Achievement of Stated Aims

Without actually using the program, and keeping your own pupils in mind, to what extent do you think the program would achieve its/ your aims and objectives? *? ? ?*

Robustness

Is it easy for the user to correct typing errors? *Yes*

Are possible errors trapped? When numerical input is required, what happens if you type in a word? *N/A*

What happens if you type in a number when a word is required? *Error trapped*

When textual input is required, what is the longest sentence you can input? Does the program crash if you enter a longer one? *N/A No*

Can you get all the way through the program without entering anything, just pressing the RETURN key each time a word, number or sentence is required? *No*

When numerical input is required, what happens if you type in very large or very small numbers? Can the program cope with an input of zero or a negative number? *N/A*

Are all non-essential keys automatically turned off by the program itself? Try pressing some wrong keys, e.g. ESCAPE BREAK SHIFT/BREAK, the CONTROL key in conjunction with any others. *No*

Figure 4.3   Assessment of 'Flowers of Crystal' Using Blease's Educational Software Selection Criteria

problematical; while these are not provided directly by the program, they would be provided by the classroom environment it creates.

The MicroSIFT questions on the accuracy and educational value of the program's content seem inappropriate for this program, and yet there can be a good deal of accurate and varied content material of great educational value in the projects and activities sponsored by the program. This problem is even more marked perhaps in the questions in the Salvas and Thomas list concerning the program having a clearly defined topic and fitting the syllabus. For most teachers these would seem to be among the most important questions in software assessment; without relevance to the curriculum educational software might be of little value indeed. For the program itself the answer to these syllabus and topic questions must be negative, and yet, as is clear from the foregoing description, the potential of the program to sponsor and support off-computer classroom activities which enhance learning in many syllabus topic areas is considerable.

The checklists provide an instrument for detailed assessment of the attributes of the package itself, and are useful as far as they go. But we need some broader way of looking critically at the software, a way which encompasses as well an assessment of the classroom learning environment engendered by the package. This includes looking not only at the experiences of students as they actually work with the program at the computer, but also at their learning activities associated with use of the program, carried out away from the computer itself.

In the next section we will look, though more briefly, at some other educational software packages, to see how well checklists enable us to say what we want to about their educational value and use.

Using Checklists to Assess Two Genetics Programs

Judith Kinnear, an Australian software author, has developed a series of packages to assist students of genetics. We shall look briefly at two of her programs, *Heredity Dog* (Kinnear, 1983) and *Catlab* (Kinnear, 1982), the first of which deals with genetics in dogs, and the second with cats. Is the animal being studied the only basis on which a teacher would make a choice between the two programs? Completing a checklist on the features of each of the packages would reveal almost no other difference between them. Having the same author, their topic areas and syllabus relevance, clarity of presentation, use of graphics and sound, standards of documentation and underlying educational philosophies are very similar. The only checklist criteria on which significant differences might appear are the suggested student age levels and the flexibility of the program for the user, since the *Catlab* program allows students to design their own genetics experiments, while the experiments available in *Heredity Dog* are a fixed set of activities in which students simply select a pair of dogs for breeding. Apart from this, the programs' assessments appear essentially identical, and a teacher might be led to think the choice between them is quite a trivial one.

Readers familiar with these programs would know that this is not in fact the case. The single criterion on which the two programs differ makes them enormously different from one another in the kinds of learning experiences they provide for students. We shall look briefly at each to illustrate this.

Heredity Dog gives the user control of the rate of progress and the sequence of progress through the program, and over the gene system to be studied, the genetic make-up of each parent, and litter size in the range two to five. All other variables are set by the program.

Students make selections from menus to determine their sequence through the program.

```
WHAT NOW?
YOU CAN . . .
        1 SEE ONE GENE IN ACTION
        2 SEE TWO GENES IN ACTION
        3 SEE SUMMARY OF LAST CROSS
        4 LOOK AT REVISION
        5 END THE PROGRAM

        TYPE 1, 2, 3, 4 OR 5
```

Figure 4.4   Menu illustrating extent of user control in 'Heredity Dog'

The genetic characteristics of a set of parents are also selected using menus.

```
CHOOSE THE PARENT DOGS . .

FIRST THE MOTHER . .
SHE CAN BE:
        1. HOMOZYGOUS BLACK
        2. HETEROZYGOUS
        3. HOMOZYGOUS BROWN

        TYPE 1, 2 OR 3
```

Figure 4.5   Menu for determining genotype of parent in 'Heredity Dog'

The genetic characteristics of the pups are determined by the program according to an appropriate model, and presented for the students. Students may obtain more than one litter from a set of parents.

The other program, *Catlab* allows users to simulate the mating of cats of any valid colour or coat pattern. Menus enable the user to specify characteristics of the cats' appearance as shown in Figure 4.6. Any number of cats up to eight can be specified.

EXCLUDING ANY WHITE AREAS WHAT IS THE COLOR OF THE FUR?
1 BLACK
2 GREY
3 BLACK AND ORANGE
4 GREY AND CREAM
5 ORANGE
6 CREAM

TYPE 1, 2, 3, 4, 5 OR 6

Figure 4.6   Part of the menu structure for adding a new cat in 'Catlab'

Any of the specified cats may be selected for breeding at any time. The user can obtain a colour-coded graphics representation of all of the cats which have been specified or a summary list of their identification numbers, sex and features (see Figure 4.7).

YOU HAVE 2 FEMALE AND 1 MALE CAT(S)
WHAT NEXT?
1 PRODUCE A LITTER OF KITTENS FROM SELECTED PARENTS
2 ADD ANOTHER CAT
3 START AGAIN
4 RECALL THE LIST OF CATS
5 END THE PROGRAM

TYPE 1, 2, 3, 4 OR 5

Figure 4.7   Menu illustrating extent of user control in 'Catlab'

The student specifies the outward appearances of the cats, but cannot assume that the cats are pure breeding so must infer their genetic make-up. This involves designing experiments to test hypotheses in ways similar to those used in real life genetics research. The manual for the package states that *Catlab* is intended to be open-ended in this way, simply acting as a vehicle for investigation in genetics. Although a number of sample investigations are suggested, in general the problem to be investigated, the starting point, the sequence of investigations, and the finishing point can all be student-defined and student-controlled. The important outcome of using the program is expected not so much to be the conclusions reached, but rather the appropriateness of the procedures used and the validity of the scientific reasoning behind the procedures.

This open-endedness of the *Catlab* package means that students must take a good deal of initiative in designing the activities, in a way that is not at all the case for students using *Heredity Dog*. *Heredity Dog* is essentially a simulation program enabling students to explore some principles of genetics within a constrained environment. In *Catlab*, on the other hand, the designer has provided students with a much broader and less structured environment in which to explore genetic ideas. The activities available to students using *Catlab* are much more varied and extensive, since the program allows students to design their own genetics experiments. Consequently, students need more background knowledge and skills to use the program with benefit. The learning activities and experiences provided by the two programs are significantly different, and in this case the checklist approach to assessment misses out almost completely on much that is very important about the software packages.

Checklists for Software Selection in Some Other Curriculum Areas

Another area in which the checklist approach is inadequate is in the selection of a utility program, such as a word processor, suitable for use in a particular school setting. Assessing several word processing packages using checklists such as those we have seen would, as was the case for the genetics programs, emphasize the similarities of the packages more than differences between them. This can make selection decisions appear trivial, when there is in fact an enormous variety in the power and the ease of use of word processors available to schools. Blease's construction, described in Chapter 3, of separate checklists for different categories of packages, while providing some help here, does not solve the problem completely. It is possible to design checklist criteria to discriminate between programs of a particular type, such as word processors, on the basis of attributes of the programs themselves, such as technical characteristics, and quality of documentation, but it is virtually impossible to consider with the checklist approach fundamental differences in the ways in which users will interact with the program, and in the experiences and the learning environment it might provide for them.

Many recent curriculum guidelines contain more than just content topics; they include as well various process-related skills as important outcomes in learning. It is thought that development of many of these can be considerably enhanced by computer-based experience, and suitable software packages are available. One example is the range of information handling packages, with which students collect, classify, interpret, organize and store data, and then interrogate it for analysis. Another is the variety of spreadsheet programs now available. A third example is provided by some of the modelling programs designed for students. While special checklists could be designed to discriminate between programs within each of these groups, these again would necessarily attend more to the technical attributes and features of the programs themselves than to the ways in which the programs might be used to develop process skills. The differences between these programs and the ways in which they might be used are often more complex or more subtle than can be adequately articulated by responding to a list of simple questions. We need a more discursive approach to making selection decisions and planning classroom use of software packages in these cases.

5 Problems with the Checklist Approach for Software Selection

Inevitably there are difficulties in designing checklists. Blease (1986) drew attention to the problem of inappropriate selection criteria and adequate explanation of these. Designing a form that can be completed in reasonable time often means simplifying the types of responses required; note for example that the Salvas and Thomas (1984) list uses mostly simple Yes/No answers. However the problems to be considered in this chapter are more fundamental than the actual design of the checklist forms.

In the literature on software assessment we have found many comments and criticisms supporting the view that checklists have serious limitations as a technique for software selection. Some criticisms of the checklist approach take the form of complaints about the application of the technique for particular types of selection problem; others are concerned with deficiencies in the criteria available for expressing opinions about packages, with their levels of generality or specificity, or with their emphasis on technical matters rather than fundamental educational ones. Since these criticisms assist in understanding some important issues, we shall examine them at some length in this chapter. Then we shall look at roles for checklists in software evaluation, and at the relationship of checklists to theoretical frameworks for considering educational software.

Limitations of the Checklist Approach

In this section we consider the major limitations of the checklist approach.

Equal Weighting of Criteria in Checklists

Winship draws attention to the constraints on expressing a view about a particular package when the criteria in the list are all equally weighted.

> One of the problems with drawing up lists of such criteria is that in many cases all criteria are given equal weighting in evaluating the software. For example, the presence or absence of colour or graphics might have no significance at all in the case of some types of software such as spreadsheets or database management systems. (Winship, 1988 p. 371)

Clearly it is difficult to indicate relative weightings for questions on a checklist, although some, such as whether the program will run on the school's make of computer, may be vastly more important than others. The problem was evidently noted by the developers of the MicroSIFT (1982) list as it allows for the reviewer to specify Higher or Lower importance ratings for items in the list.

Checklists do not Allow for Different Teaching Strategies

Winship continues:

> Another problem is when the criteria do not allow for variation in the teaching strategy. Often criteria are designed to be applied to all types of software regardless of the teaching strategy. The criteria for judging a tutorial should be different from those used for judging a spreadsheet or a word processing package. (Winship, 1988 p. 371)

This comment is consistent with the development by Blease (1986) of additional criteria for different software types. The teaching strategy problem is outlined particularly clearly by an example, the case of selecting software for teaching writing, from Miller and Burnett.

> The majority of available software falls into the first category, grammar drill and practise. This is paradoxical as we can find no current approach to composition instruction that advocates teaching grammar in isolation. . . . Using many of today's software evaluation schemes, grammar drill and practise programs would receive high ratings. After all they possess specific skills,

quality graphics, give instant feedback, and keep records of students' performance. That they seem to match no current theory of composition instruction seems to highlight our concern for asking more fundamental questions. (Miller and Burnett, 1986 p. 164)

And again with software selection for teaching reading:

> The debate between scholars advocating a subskill or a holistic approach to the teaching of reading is an honest one . . . However, in computer-aided instruction, the issue of applying reading theory to software programs is addressed infrequently . . . Moreover, many of the existing guidelines dictate that software will be evaluated by subskill criteria by virtue of their wording. (Miller and Burnett, 1986 p. 160)

These writers argue that the checklist designer makes

> . . . the mistake of devising one set of evaluation criteria, and the wording of the guidelines creates a situation where software that conforms to an implied theory is rated highly. Other software, which might be congruent with a theoretical position different from the one implied, is rated poorly. (Miller and Burnett, 1986 p. 163)

Additional Criteria for Particular Situations

We noted earlier that Blease (1986) saw a need to develop different sets of criteria for selection of different types of software. Komoski (1987) argues for the development of different sets of criteria for selection of software for different discipline areas.

> Although educational software is a unique medium, it is not so unique that it can be excused from being judged by the canons of good teaching and the established principles of learning — including the degree to which it validly and accurately reflects the best of current thinking within a discipline. For this reason . . . it is important for evaluators of educational software to move beyond the assumption that all software can be evaluated by means of a set of generic criteria. The time has come to move to the development of specific criteria for

judging the quality of software in separate disciplines. (Komoski, 1987 p. 403)

Discussing the MicroSIFT checklist, Langhorne *et al.*, suggest that, despite its extent, it may not enable reviewers to say the things they consider important.

> Districts may wish to enhance this form by adding questions that address some specific concerns of potential users, e.g. 'How many minutes are required for average use?' 'Is student involvement active or passive?' 'Describe the social characteristics of the program (competitive or cooperative). Is that positive or negative?' 'Is the program most appropriate for individual, small group, or large-group use?' . . . While the criteria checklist of such a form is useful in guiding an evaluator through the examination of a software package, the most informative part of the form is that which requires a summarization of the strengths and weaknesses of the package. (Langhorne *et al.*, 1989 p. 35)

In assessing software for teaching reading, Miller and Burnett (1986) also want to add to the typical checklist criteria, but they want to add only one question. They suggest a two level process for selection of software to help children learn to read. The first level would consist of a single question: 'How do you think reading should be taught?' and a second level could focus on various technical concerns.

Technical and Educational Criteria

Many of the questions in the checklists concern matters which would not be considered significant in the same way in the selection of other resource materials for teaching, such as textbooks, kits, and so on. Matters equivalent to program robustness, ease of startup, clarity of instructions for use, error trapping, and so on, while still valid considerations (as Templeton's list of 'nasties' in Chapter 2 makes clear), would not be to the fore in teachers' minds as they browse through books or other print resources. Of course a book which is poorly designed or difficult to use, or contains spelling errors, incorrect use of upper and lower case letters, or poor editing, would be rejected, but these 'technical' matters are noted almost incidentally as teachers consider more educational criteria, such as curriculum and pedagogical issues, as they examine a new resource.

The relative ease with which technical criteria can be developed, and the difficult, almost impossible, challenge of devising checklist items that assess educational value in a program, have resulted in the lists being dominated by technical questions. This technical emphasis is reflected in statements such as the following.

> . . . the process for evaluating microcomputer software must be structured, systematic, and thorough to ensure that software is not only appropriate for the curriculum and instructionally sound, but also effective in its use of relevant computer capabilities. (Langhorne *et al.*, 1989 pp. 32–3)

Many writers are critical of this emphasis. We cite some examples here. Miller and Burnett criticize one checklist as

> . . . similar to those found in other articles focusing on this topic in that most of the advice concerns issues related to hardware, record keeping, previewing privileges and presentation format. (Miller and Burnett, 1986 p. 159)

Other criticisms include:

> The checklist approach to software evaluation has been challenged because products that meet certain technical criteria do not necessarily accomplish their educational objectives. (OTA, 1988 p. 136)

> It is relatively easy to design the sheet when a 'good/fair/poor/ NA' response is required, and hence the technical sections of the sheet seem reasonable. It is far more difficult to characterize adequately educational criteria so that they may be answered in the same fashion. (Winship, 1988 p. 372)

> A major difficulty in composing guidelines for software evaluation is that it is relatively easy to specify trivial criteria, such as those concerning screen presentation, the use of sound and graphics, positive reinforcement for the user and the inclusion of a scoring or record-keeping system, and then to rate the programs on these criteria. Although they are important because of their effects on user's motivation and interest, such criteria do not touch the central learning issues with which education is concerned. (Johnston, 1987 p. 44)

The really challenging aspects of selecting software for use with students are not technical ones at all. Rather they are concerned with classroom management, curriculum integration, resource acquisition, and questions of pedagogy and learning.

Formal and Informal Review

Heller (1991) distinguishes between 'informal' review, not unlike a book review, and 'formal' review, which uses a checklist. Although she clearly sees formal review as the most desirable, she notes limitations of the technique in the selection of the most recent and innovative software.

> Even formal reviews are not the complete answer to software review. Especially in today's world where new technological approaches such as hypermedia and artificial reality are capable of bringing new forms of educational software into the classroom, it is quite possible for a piece of software to be excellent in ways which are not delineated by the guidelines. (Heller, 1991 p. 286)

Elsewhere Heller acknowledges the value of 'informal' reviewing when she cites the report of the OTA (1988) acknowledging the opinions of teachers working without checklists, stating that these teachers'

> . . . views are often the most credible, even if their assessments do not conform to rigorous methodology (Heller, 1991 p. 286)

Questioning the Overall Suitability of Checklists for Software Selection

Johnston (1987) is one of the few writers we have found who actually questions the suitability for software selection of the checklist approach as such, including the following criticism in an account of a teacher professional development course on software selection. '. . . The effectiveness and appropriateness of the checklist as a means of evaluating is not considered' (Johnston, 1987 p. 43).
Johnston continues:

> No evaluation can predict how a given piece of software will actually be used within the classroom as this depends on the individual factors of the teaching approach adopted, the nature of the curriculum into which the software is introduced, the

management strategies employed, and the needs and reactions of the users themselves. . . . What happens when the program is selected for use in learning depends as much on the uses to which it is put, that is on how it is exploited within the curriculum and the learning environment, as on its inherent design. (Johnston, 1987 pp. 45–6)

This view is endorsed by Smith and Keep.

It was conventional to assume that objectives laid down by the software designers were understood, accepted and shared by teachers (and students!), and that the quality of a package could be determined according to the extent to which these objectives were attained by appropriate target students. . . . One practical result of this was a variety of detailed checklists . . . There are real problems with the input–output model, even where teachers have the experience, expertise and time to apply exhaustive checklists . . . Most formal education takes place within the context of an extremely complex social environment, where the variables relevant to the relationship between treatments and outcomes may not even be clearly recognizable, let alone capable of precise operational definition or effective experimental control. . . . Teachers and students may find objectives, purposes and applications for the technology which were unthought of by its originators. (Smith and Keep, 1988 p. 153)

We found in the last chapter that the general purpose checklist approach to assessment, while helpful to a certain extent, is not adequate to convey some of the most important features of educational software packages. In the case *of Flowers of Crystal*, assessment checklists fail to convey the real educational power of the package as they do not enable us to describe the learning environment away from the computer engendered in the classroom by the program. In other cases this approach trivializes important differences between superficially similar programs, or oversimplifies other more complex issues of selection and use.

Checklists for Software Evaluation

Adding more questions to the checklists or making them more sophisticated in design might improve them, but this would not really overcome the fundamental problem. The problem is this. The checklist approach as such is not really suitable for the task of assessment of software for *selection* purposes.

Is there then any role at all for the checklist approach to assessment of educational software? We believe that there is, but that the role in which it is most useful is in the *formative evaluation* of software, not in selection. During trialling of a package, a checklist of questions written specifically for that package can be of great assistance to trials teachers in assessing whether the program under development is technically sound, and whether the package can in fact achieve its stated aims. In this case the checklist can be developed using questions that arise specifically from the stated aims of the package, and which concern technical criteria which are particularly relevant to its presentation. An example of such a checklist, prepared in 1988 by Flavell, co-ordinator of a development team working on a package called *ELGAME*, later published as *TELETOM: A Telecommunications Adventure* (Flavell, Gomberg, and Squires, 1989), is shown in Figure 5.1.

Notice that the problem described by Blease (1986), the inclusion in checklists of many criteria inappropriate to the program under consideration, no longer applies. The checklist for program evaluation is designed specifically for assessment of that program.

Past confusion of evaluation with selection has resulted in the use of checklists for both purposes. On Blease's list the question associated with achievement of stated aims, which tries to cover both evaluation and selection criteria simultaneously, illustrates this confusion: 'Without actually using the program, and keeping your own pupils in mind, to what extent do you think the program would achieve its/your aims and objectives?' (Blease, 1986 p. 85).

Do checklists have any role to play in summative evaluation, the assessment or review of a completed package? They have certainly been used extensively for this purpose in the past, and clearly have some role to play here. To be of most use in this context a checklist needs to be as closely tailored as possible to the package under review, and needs to be supplemented with more discursive comments in which educational issues can be addressed in a useful way.

There are already a number of frameworks or paradigms for thinking about educational computing, but none has paid attention to the distinction between the processes of software evaluation and selection. The resulting confusion has led, we believe, to the use of the checklist approach in software selection as well as in software evaluation, with negative effect on the development of effective procedures for software selection.

BT/CIC ELGAME TRIALS

If the program was trialled on more than one class, please use a separate sheet for each
    group.
Leave blank any questions you prefer not to answer.

Details of class
Year/age:
Number in class:
Number of girls:
Ability (top/middle/bottom/mixed):
Number of sessions spent using the material:
Duration of each session:
Familiarity of students with use of computers:

Actual use of software
How many computers were used?
In what subject was it used? (Science/Physics/Electronics/IT/Computer Studies/other)
In conjunction with which course was it used? (e.g.GCSE Nuffield Co-ordinated Science, MEG
    GCSE Electronics, etc.)
Was it used in context as part of one of the above courses? (yes/no)
Was it used to introduce a topic/as revision/other?

Approach using the software and class organization
Was the software appropriate to the age of the trials group?
If not, for what age/ability range would it be appropriate?
How often are computers used with this group of pupils in these lessons normally?
(always/often/sometimes/occasionally/never)
Did the use of the computer enhance the teaching of this topic? (yes/no)
Did using the materials create any special problems? (yes/no)
If yes, please expand.
Is the software relevant to the curriculum? (yes/no)

Presentation of software and accompanying materials
Is the 'game' format appropriate to teach this topic? (yes/no)
How would you judge the content? (very interesting/interesting/average/poor/very poor)
How easy did the pupils find the program? (5 easy—1 impossible)
Did you find any 'bugs' or confusing instructions in the program? (yes/no)
If so, please expand.
Did you use the accompanying pupil worksheets? (yes/no)
If so, how useful are they? (5 very—1 useless)
How useful is the information booklet? (5 very—1 useless)
Have you any suggestions for improving
    (a) the user installation instructions
    (b) the worksheets
    (c) the booklet?
Have you any suggestions for additional worksheets?

Overall reaction
Reaction of pupils:
Reaction of staff:
Would you buy it?

Please use the back of the form to add any further comments you would like to make.
Thank you for your time and effort in filling in this evaluation sheet.

Figure 5.1 Trials Checklist for the ELGAME *Program*

Relationship of Checklists to Theoretical Frameworks

Checklists are developed, whether consciously or inadvertently, from theoretical frameworks for thinking about the use of computers in education. The checklists carry implicit sets of values and priorities, and these necessarily affect the scope and perspectives of our thinking about educational software. Referring to the MicroSIFT checklist, Langhorne *et al.* suggest this relationship with the statement: 'The format of this instrument provides a framework that causes the evaluator to systematically examine software for qualities . . .' (Langhorne *et al.*, 1989 p. 34), and Miller and Burnett give a clear example of the importance of the interaction. 'When evaluation criteria, such as the list proposed by Krause, are accepted by reading educators, then it is not surprising to see software designers tailor their programs accordingly' (Miller and Burnett, 1986 p. 160).

Preece and Jones emphasize –

> the importance of a sound framework in which teachers can develop selection skills so that they can go beyond the superficial technical features of the programs to consider whether the underlying pedagogy is sound and suited to their needs. (Preece and Jones, 1985 p. 10)

Acknowledging the importance of this relationship between practical approaches to software selection and theoretical frameworks for thinking about educational software, we examine in detail some relevant theoretical frameworks in Chapter 6.

6   Frameworks for Studying Educational Software

Numerous attempts have been made since the introduction of computers into education to devise frameworks so that the designers and users of educational software might have systematic ways of thinking about their tasks. These attempts have been prompted by the desire to assist not only in software development, but also in description, discussion, comparison, selection and evaluation of educational software, and in understanding the role educational computing might have in wider educational contexts.

Many of these frameworks have taken the form of classification systems based on categories to which software packages might be assigned. Other frameworks have focused on the roles that software is intended to fulfil. Yet others have attempted to relate software to commonly accepted educational rationales. These three approaches — based on categorization, roles, and educational rationales — are discussed and critically reviewed in this chapter with reference to examples of well-known frameworks. Many frameworks have been developed, and we do not claim to have completed a comprehensive review; the chosen examples are representative of the essential features of each of these approaches.

Classification by Application Type

A very simplistic but commonly used approach distinguishes between two types of educational software: content-free software and subject-specific software. Content-free (another term in frequent use is 'generic') software is thought of in terms of the tasks that it can perform; for example word processors can be used to manipulate text, information handling packages can be used to interrogate data, spreadsheets can be used to perform extensive and complicated calculations.

Content free software is not specifically designed for a particular topic or area in the curriculum, but might be used for different purposes by teachers of different subjects. Thus the same information handling package might be used by a history teacher to explore local census records, and by a chemistry teacher to investigate patterns in the periodic table of chemical elements. In contrast, subject-specific software includes all packages designed to be used in the teaching and learning of specific topics, in particular curriculum or subject areas. Examples of such packages include simulation programs for science topics, foreign language practice programs, and arithmetic drill programs.

There have been many attempts to develop more sophisticated frameworks based on classification by application type. Some representative examples are shown in Table 6.1.

It is interesting to note that this approach to classification has been popular throughout the development of the use of computers in education, and, as can be seen from the table, it remains contemporary.

Beech (1983) provides an early example of this approach with the identification of the following 'styles': slide show, in which the software presents a sequence of demonstration materials; testing, in which tests are administered and marked; drill and practice exercises; tutorial, defined as an interactive dialogue of teaching and testing; command mode, in which the user has well-developed control over the operation of the package; numerical simulation; and decision tree, in which the user is progressively confronted with a series of choices, and games. Wellington (1985) attempts to provide a more organized system of classification by adopting a two tier approach, with software categories grouped under four headings; teaching programs, learning programs, tools, and open-ended use.

Later examples of this approach are provided in reports published by the USA Office of Technology Assessment (1988) and the Organization for Economic Co-operation and Development (1989). The OTA report gives a list of software categories that is essentially composed of two sub-groups; one sub-group is concerned with categories of educational applications (rote drill, skills practice, tutorial, concept demonstration, concept development, and hypothesis testing), and the other with categories of software design (educational games, simulations, and tool programs). The OECD identifies the following categories which are mainly based on application types, although 'exploration and discovery' is included as a final category: drill and practice, tutorial, intelligent

Table 6.1   Education software frameworks based on classification by application type

Author(s)	Date	Classification types
Beech	1983	Slide show, testing, drill and practice exercises, tutorial, command mode, numerical simulation, decision tree, and games.
Hofmeister	1984	Programmed-instruction-based CAI (drill and practice, tutorial), artificial intelligence based CAI, simulation orientated CAI, tool applications.
Salvas and Thomas	1984	Information retrieval, drill and practice, games, modelling, simulation, tutorial, application packages, and teaching support.
Wellington	1985	Teaching programs (drill and practice, tutorial, electronic teaching aid), learning programs (educational games, adventure games, simulations), tools (information retrieval, word processing), and open-ended use (*Logo*).
Newman	1988	Word processing, simulations, adventure programs, information retrieval, problem solving, drill and practice, tutorial, spreadsheets, control applications, communications, teacher productivity tools.
USA Office of Technology Assessment	1988	Rote drill, skills practice, tutorial, concept demonstration, concept development, hypothesis testing, educational games, simulations, and tool programs.
Organization for Economic Co-operation and Development	1989	Drill and practice, tutorial, intelligent tutoring systems, simulation and model building, problem solving, educational games, information retrieval and database management, word processing, application programs, computer managed learning, microcomputer-based instrumentation, and exploration and discovery.
Pelgrum and Plomp	1991	Drill and practice, tutorial programs, word processing, painting and drawing, music composition, simulation, recreational games, educational games, programming languages, spreadsheet, mathematics graphing, statistics, data base, lab interfaces, programs to control devices, programs to control interactive video, CAD/CAM, CAI authoring language, item banks, record/score tests, grade book, computer communication, and tools/utilities.

tutoring systems, simulation and model building, problem solving, educational games, information retrieval and database management, word processing, application programs, computer managed learning, microcomputer-based instrumentation, and exploration and discovery. Pelgrum and Plomp (1991) provide a contemporary example which lists twenty-three categories, indicating that as the range and diversity of software increases, frameworks based on the classification by application type will need to become even more extensive.

Experience has shown that reference to software categories can be useful for describing in an overall way the style or structure of a package. Although, for example, spreadsheet packages vary considerably one from another in matters of detail, they do have in common an overall structure and style of use, so if a new program is described as a spreadsheet this gives us some useful information about what to expect of the program. In addition it is relatively simple to classify software using this approach.

Despite the apparent utility and simplicity of this approach there are three clearly identifiable problems related to classification of educational software in terms of application type:

(i)   The criteria for delineation of categories are often implicit, without a clear rationale for their choice. Application categories corresponding to educational approaches, such as drill and practice, are often mixed with categories based on software function, such as word processing. Decisions about which types to include depend on perceptions of what is significant in the use of educational software. For instance, Beech appears to put a strong emphasis on the notion of the computer as a surrogate teacher, while the OECD provides a far more eclectic set of categories. While the types suggested by Beech are similar in character, the types given by the OECD are quite different, leading to the possibility of inappropriate comparisons. For example, is it sensible to compare software corresponding to two of the categories suggested by the OECD — a computer managed learning system and an educational game?

(ii)   As experience and the range of uses of software in education increases the range of categories needed will also increase, as illustrated by the very large classification set used by Pelgrum and Plomp (1991). Classification by software type is very time sensitive. Given the rapid way in which both the character and range of possible uses of software in education is changing, frameworks based on this approach can become redundant very quickly, implying a constant need for revision and up-dating.

(iii)   With the move to integrated software environments which provide linked access to a number of applications, some more recent packages used in education do not fall neatly into any one classification. This concern is particularly acute when commercial software packages are being assessed for use in education. How should an integrated software package such as *Microsoft Works* (consisting of a linked spreadsheet, word processor and database package) be classified? This issue is also becoming important with respect to packages designed specifically for education. For example, *Priority* (Flavell, Gomberg, and Squires, 1993) is an educational package based on the use of a custom designed planning simulation from which data can be exported to commonly available spreadsheets. How would this package be classified?

From these criticisms it can be seen, that while frameworks based on classification by application type may be easy to develop, they must be used with caution. The categories within such frameworks, which may be quite different in scope and origin, are frequently specified with reference to unstated criteria. If the framework is not very recent the categories may not represent current ideas and practices. And the move to integrated, multi-faceted software environments makes the categorization of software increasingly problematic. At best, frameworks based on classification by software type are of limited use; at worst they lead to confusion through inappropriate categorical comparisons.

Classification by Educational Role

Some frameworks for describing software have used educational role as a basis for classification. Here the emphasis is on the way that software is intended to perform; the definition is in terms of what the software is capable of doing rather than of characteristics of the user. These frameworks are oriented towards software design issues, with issues of cognition and pedagogy rather more subsidiary. A classic example of this approach is provided by Taylor (1980), who described three roles for educational software: tutor, tool, and tutee. Software operating as a tutor is intended to provide a surrogate teacher, in which the '. . . computer presents some subject material, the student responds, the computer evaluates the response, and, from the results of the evaluation, determines what to present next (Taylor, 1980 p. 3). Well-known examples of this approach are drill and practice exercises and adaptive tutorial programs.

The tool mode is characterized by the computer's performance of tedious labour intensive activities, enabling the learner to concentrate on essential concepts without being distracted by the demands of 'inauthentic' labour. As Taylor remarks '. . . to function as a tool, the classroom computer need only have some useful capability programmed into it such as statistical analysis, super calculation, or word processing' (Taylor, 1980 p. 4).

Other examples of software used in this way include graphics packages to draw multiple graphs, data logging software to collect and record repetitive experimental data over extended time periods, and information handling packages to interrogate large data files.

The tutee mode refers to provision by the computer of environments in which learners can 'teach' the computer through expressing their own ideas and solutions to problems. The best known example of this approach is the programming language *Logo*, designed to provide learners with opportunities to explore and construct microworlds by writing and debugging procedures. Developing and testing models by using a computer-based modelling package would also correspond to the tutee role.

O'Shea and Self (1983) describe software acting in the roles of surrogate teacher and learning resource. Software acting as a surrogate teacher is responsible for prescribing tasks and for presenting a defined body of knowledge to students; as a resource there is a far greater emphasis on learning by involvement. Self (1985) develops this framework further by regarding educational software as an example of an educational medium. This allows him to take Rowntree's analysis (1982) of the functions of educational media as the basis for developing a set of detailed roles for educational software. Rowntree lists six functions: engage the student's motivation, recall earlier learning, provide new learning stimuli, activate the student's response, give speedy feedback, and encourage appropriate practice. Self suggests two more roles (sequence learning and provide a resource) to propose a version of Rowntree's list which is specifically adapted to educational software. Seven roles for educational software result from this adaptation, as shown in Table 6.2. Examples of software associated with each role are given in the table to illustrate the nature of Self's framework.

Frameworks based on roles for educational software are founded on the premise that the scope and nature of the software environment defines educational possibilities. The focus is not the learner, with personal learning needs, or the teacher with perceptions of appropriate curricula and pedagogies. The focus is the role that the software has been designed to play, and in this sense the emphasis is on the designer, without any particular attempt to relate the perspectives of the designer to those of the student and the teacher. Self emphasizes this principle in his introduction to his book, *Microcomputers and Education: a critical appraisal of educational software*:

Table 6.2 *Educational software roles identified by Self (1985)*

Role	Example(s) of software associated with role
Engaging motivation	Adventure games, computer games.
Providing new stimuli	Programs which 'mimic' the real world — computer-based versions of existing problem solving games (for example *Hunt the Thimble*), adventure game representations of real world activities (for example an archeological dig), 'cut down' versions of major software applications (for example simulations of vehicle licensing data-processing systems), and simulations of scientific phenomena.
Activating pupil response	Programs which present students with a challenge (for example *Snooker* which presents the student with the challenge of potting the ball by estimating appropriate angles).
Giving information	Drills, tutorials, information handling packages, and query languages (for example *Prolog*).
Encouraging practice	Drills.
Sequencing learning	Tutorial packages.
Providing a resource	Programs without pre-defined ways in which they should be used, for example *Logo*.

> My focus is on educational software as technical objects. While this software does cause us to rethink the nature of education . . . it now seems possible to limit ourselves to the software itself without a lengthy, and yet superficial discussion of education. . . . Books exist, for example, on commercial software, legal software and medical software and their authors do not worry unduly about the nature of commerce, law and medicine. Likewise, I shall not address myself directly to the nature of education. Effective computer-aided learning depends upon the design of good educational software, so there will be enough to think about. (Self, 1985 p. 21)

Inherent in this approach is a danger of ignoring important issues of learning and teaching, with education seen in terms of what software can offer rather than software seen in terms of educational needs and possibilities.

Classification by Educational Rationale

One of the most respected and used frameworks for educational software is provided by Kemmis, Atkin, and Wright. This was developed during a large scale evaluation of the UK National Development Programme in Computer Assisted Learning (1973–75). The framework is based on the proposition of three paradigms of education '. . . through which we may grasp the major ways in which the developers of computer assisted learning conceive the curriculum task' (Kemmis, Atkin, and Wright, 1977 p. 24).

These paradigms are labelled as instructional, revelatory, and conjectural. The developers of this framework tentatively suggest a fourth paradigm — the emancipatory paradigm — which originates from the notion of the computer as a labour saving tool, and which only exists in conjunction with one of the other three.

Associated with the instructional paradigm is the mastery of content, with subject matter seen as the object of learning. Instruction is rationalized using such techniques as sequencing, presentation and feedback reinforcement. Software associated with this paradigm aims explicitly to teach material, usually by breaking it up into small parts and presenting these to students. There are opportunities for the students to respond to test questions and to receive feedback on the accuracy of their responses. The software assumes the responsibility for presenting content, providing feedback, and allocating tasks. These programs cover a wide variety of topic areas from drill programs in word recognition or arithmetic problems to intelligent tutoring systems designed to teach medical students to diagnose bacterial infections.

The revelatory paradigm emphasizes learning by discovery and developing an intuitive feel for the field of study; the student is seen as the prime focus. Software is used to provide environments for exploration and discovery. The classic examples of this paradigm are simulations, where a computer-based model is used to simulate a real-life environment, often involving situations which might otherwise be difficult to study in a classroom. Students investigate the model by entering data and observing results generated by the program, and key ideas and concepts may be revealed as the students work with the software. Many simulation programs have been developed, concerning a very wide range of situations. Some examples are simulations of a nuclear power station, genetic inheritance, economic situations and the ecology of a pond.

The conjectural paradigm includes the articulation and manipulation of ideas and hypothesis testing. The curriculum emphasis of this approach is the development of understanding through the active construction of knowledge. Software is seen as providing environments for articulating and exploring ideas through the creation of models, programs, plans and conceptual structures. Software associated with the conjectural paradigm enables students to explore a topic by formulating and testing their own hypotheses about the situation or system being studied. Examples of software appropriate to this paradigm are modelling packages which not only allow students to input data to a model, but enable them to actually modify the model itself and observe the effects. Computer-based microworlds which enable students to express their ideas and construct solutions to problems by changing the state of a computational object through programming, such as the heading and position of a turtle in *Logo*, provide further examples of software associated with this paradigm.

The emancipatory paradigm is concerned with software which exploits the capacity of the computer to process large amounts of data and perform many operations very quickly, to save students from spending time on laborious tasks that are necessary but incidental to their learning. For example, students might use the computer's power for fast arithmetic calculation in a program to analyze data for science experiments, enabling them to concentrate on the scientific part of their work. In itself this paradigm is not directly concerned with an educational rationale; rather it is seen as a way of facilitating one or more of the other three paradigms. Kemmis *et al.* (1977) describe software used in an emancipatory fashion as obviating 'inauthentic labour', labour that does not contribute directly to the intended (or authentic) educational task in hand, but which nevertheless needs to be completed. Thus information handling software may be used to interrogate census records to identify patterns of historical development (a revelatory use of software) with the software rapidly sorting and searching large amounts of data in a way which would be impossible by hand (an emancipatory use).

Although this approach is sixteen years old at the time of writing, the framework developed by Kemmis and his colleagues still provides a useful approach. This is noted by Watson in her assessment of the paradigm's values and limitations: 'Although not necessarily totally adequate, it does provide one of the few attempts at a more rigorous look at the variety of learning activities within the definition of CAL, and thus is a useful reference base' (Watson, 1987 p. 15).

However it is important to be aware of some limitations of this approach:

(i) There is a tendency to regard software as belonging exclusively to one paradigm. This cannot be the case for the emancipatory paradigm, as this applies by definition only in tandem with one of the three others. Further, the same software can be associated with more than one of the other paradigms. For example, the use of information retrieval packages may support both pattern recognition (revelatory paradigm) and model building (conjectural paradigm). Associating a package with only one paradigm can lead to a constrained view of the educational possibilities of the software.

(ii) Clearly a serious attempt has been made to address curriculum issues by identifying relevant educational paradigms, but there is no consideration of the learning process.

A Critical Reflection on Existing Software Classifications

Awareness of the shortcomings of the frameworks described in the previous sections has led to the development of expanded and more sophisticated adaptations of these frameworks. In some cases these consist of amalgamations of frameworks, in attempts to improve them by expansion and adaptation.

The original framework described by Kemmis and his colleagues provides an example. MacDonald, Atkin, Jenkins and Kemmis (1977) explore the relationship between the four paradigms and a typology of student-computer assisted learning interactions derived from the research literature on the cognitive effects of computer assisted learning. This typology consists of five types of interaction: recognition (A), recall (B), reconstructive understanding or comprehension (C), global reconstructive or intuitive understanding (D), and constructive understanding (E). Figure 6.1 represents the range of interactions between each paradigm and the various interaction types, indicating that there are correlations between the educational paradigms and the various learning processes. In effect, the second criticism made in the previous section is addressed by considering the relationship between typical student-computer assisted learning interactions and paradigms of education; software classification from a curriculum perspective is related to software classification from a learning perspective. A more comprehensive framework has been developed, with more scope to assist critical thinking and discussion about educational software. Support for this approach can be found in recent literature. Underwood and Underwood (1990) state that the four paradigms can be clearly related to Gagne's (1970) four conditions of learning (intellectual learning, cognitive learning, verbal information learning, and motor skill learning). Sewell (1990) also emphasizes the need to consider the relationships between

Paradigm	Interaction type				
	A	B	C	D	E
Instructional	◀ - -	- - - - - -	- - ● - -	- - ▶	
Revelatory			◀ - -	- - ● - -	- - ▶
Conjectural				◀ - -	- - - ●
Emancipatory					

Figure 6.1   *Possible relations between paradigms and interaction types — after MacDonald,*
Atkin, Jenkins and Kemmis (1977)
(Critical points of interaction are denoted by '●')

these and similar paradigms and theories of learning. However, this expanded approach still provides an incomplete description of the rich set of interactions that are possible when software is used in a classroom. While the relationship between learning processes and curriculum design has now been addressed, other possible interactions, particularly those between approaches to computer related pedagogy and learning, are not considered.

A framework consisting of an amalgam of others is provided by Chandler (1984). He proposes a framework comprising software application categories (tutorial, games, simulation games, experimental simulation, content free tools, programming languages) linked to software models (hospital, funfair, drama, laboratory, resource centre, and workshop) as shown in Figure 6.2. For example, the software application type 'games', is linked to the funfair model. While this attempt is imaginative, it illustrates the difficulty of combining frameworks effectively. There is confusion in defining the links between application categories and models. In some cases the link is described in terms of the function that the computer would play; for example, the link between games and the funfair model involves describing the computer

Program ◀ − − − − − − − − THE LOCUS OF CONTROL − − − − − − − ▶ User					
Tutorial	**Games**	**Simulation games**	**Experimental simulation**	**Content free tools**	**Programming languages**
Programmed instruction Drill and practice	Computer as player or referee	Computer as game world: e.g. Empire-style games and the 'Adventure' genre	Mathematic-ally based models of processes such as scientific experiments	word processors sound and graphics manipulators data bases scientific instruments control technology	Logo BASIC Smalltalk
Hospital Model: User as patient	Funfair Model: User as Emulator	Drama Model: User as Role-player	Laboratory Model: User as Tester	Resource Centre Model: User as Artist or Researcher	Workshop Model: User as Inventor

Figure 6.2   A framework for studying educational software (Chandler, 1984)

as a player or referee. In other cases the link is implied by giving examples of typical applications; for example the link between content free tools and the resource centre model is described in terms of a list of relevant software and hardware (word processors, sound and graphics manipulators, data bases, scientific instruments, and control technology). The reader is left with a feeling that the framework has some interesting ideas to offer, but that it does not provide a consistent and rigorous approach.

It is clear that when frameworks are combined to develop a more sophisticated one, problems arise in dealing with interactions between the foundation frameworks. In the next chapter we shall introduce a new framework or paradigm for thinking about educational software. This paradigm is based on the interactions between the student, the teacher and the designer. It is intended to be comprehensive and to assist in identifying relevant issues in the selection, use, design and discussion of educational software. Our approach is not as concerned with classification of the software itself as previous frameworks have been; it focuses less on characteristics and attributes which describe and distinguish software packages themselves, and more on issues which seem important when software is used in learning situations.

7   A Perspectives Interactions Paradigm for Studying Educational Software

It is quite clear that the development of effective educational software assessment tools is regarded by teachers and advisers as important; the large number of attempts to develop and refine both checklists for software assessment and frameworks for software classification bears witness to a strongly perceived need. However despite the effort which has been involved in developing these tools, there have been omissions and inadequacies in the approaches to date, as highlighted by the discussion in the previous chapters. Checklists are unable to deal with essential issues of teaching and learning, core justifications for the use of educational software, and show inappropriate emphases on easily assessed technical features. Frameworks have failed to provide comprehensive and coherent models of computer-assisted learning; classifications by software type consist of *ad hoc* categories which are not defined with specific reference to educational issues, roles for software focus on software features at the expense of consideration of the characteristics of teachers and learners, and frameworks based on educational rationales stress general curriculum issues without an in-depth consideration of individual approaches to learning. It is evident that there is a need to develop a more comprehensive paradigm for the assessment, study and discussion of educational software.

In this chapter we propose a paradigm which facilitates a comprehensive and principled assessment of educational software, and which is designed to address some of the limitations of previous approaches. We wish to shift the focus in software selection away from attributes of the software itself, and towards a more comprehensive and balanced emphasis on the *use* of software to enhance teaching and learning. We might think of it as a change from asking questions like, 'What does this package do?' and 'How does this program run?' to thinking 'What kinds of learning experiences might be set up or assisted by this package?' and 'What approaches to teaching fit this package?'.

A Perspectives Interactions Paradigm

There are various people associated with the design and use of educational software — students, teachers, programmers, advisers, graphics artists, program designers, writers and publishers. We identify three 'actors' as being of principal importance: the student(s), the teacher, and the designer.

The perspectives of these three major actors are implicit in existing frameworks. Classification of software by application type implies a design perspective through its focus on types of software, classification by software role also implies a design perspective, and the educational rationales framework implies a teacher perspective through its focus on curriculum. The inadequacy of these frameworks indicates that a simple focus on one (or more) perspectives is unable to provide the basis for a satisfactory paradigm.

On reflection the reason for this is evident. The use of educational software is essentially concerned with three issues: how students' learning can be improved by using software, how teachers use software to improve and extend their teaching, and how teachers and students interact in classrooms in which software is being used. Let us look at these in terms of the three major actors we have introduced. How students use software can be thought of in terms of students' relationships to the structure and content of the software as provided by the designer, or, put more succinctly, the issues relate to the interaction between the perspective on the software of the designer and that of the student. Similarly, how teachers use software relates to the interaction between the perspective on the software of the designer and that of the teacher. Issues concerned with classroom climate and activities relate to the interaction between the perspectives of the teacher and the student. The focus of our paradigm is the *interactions* between the perspectives of the three actors. We think that many of the inadequacies of frameworks developed previously result from failure to address these interactions.

We propose a paradigm which is based on consideration of the three interactions between the perspectives of pairs of the major actors: a designer and student perspectives interaction, a designer and teacher

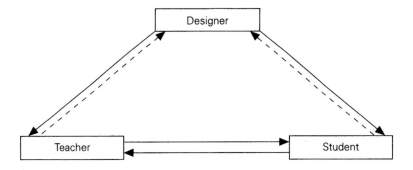

Figure 7.1   The basis of the perspectives interactions paradigm

perspectives interaction, and a teacher and student perspectives inter-action. It is interesting to note that the adapted framework described by McDonald *et al.* (1977) is based on the notion of interaction. In this case the interaction is between views of the curriculum (expressed as paradigms for computer-assisted learning) and the learning process (expressed as five different learning processes). This could be inter-preted as an interaction with specific aspects relating to the teacher (views of the curriculum) and the student (learning processes). In a limited sense this framework is a forerunner to the paradigm which we propose. However, our paradigm is far more comprehensive, enabling consideration of all issues that pertain to all three of the actors, through studying the interactions between the perspectives of pairs of them. The basic structure of this framework is shown in Figure 7.1.

As can be seen from Figure 7.1 we have identified the teacher-student perspectives interaction as bi-directional, since the interaction is between two 'live' actors. In this case the 'interaction' between the perspectives of the actors is manifest in quite direct two-way physical and social interactions between the actors themselves as they particip-ate in classroom activities together, the behaviour of each affecting and being affected by that of the other. However, both the designer-teacher and designer-student perspectives interactions are different in this respect. In each case the interaction is between the perspective of a 'live' actor (student or teacher) and that of a passive actor (designer). The interactions here cannot be as direct in nature. Once the software is written the direct involvement of the designer ends. However, the perspective of the designer interacts with the perspectives of the other two actors. The perspective of the designer is expressed in terms of soft-ware which has incorporated in it the assumptions and the intentions of the designer. Thus the link from designer to student is in a fundamental sense a static link; anything the designer wishes to provide has to be implicit in the design of the software as normally the designer will not have the opportunity to interact directly with the student. If software were only ever used as intended by the designer, the link from the student or teacher to designer would be redundant. However, in an important but subtle way, this is not the case, and this is indicated by dotted interaction lines in Figure 7.1. Educational software is very often used by students and teachers in ways unforeseen by the designer. Indeed, this 'subversive' use has led to some of the most exciting and innovative uses of educational software. This possibility can make selection of educational software a much more complex process.

It is worth considering the designer-student and designer-teacher links in more detail. Norman (1983) introduces the notion of the software designer's mental model of the user's mental model of a program, in addition to the rather simpler notions of the separate user's model and designer's model. The notion of the designer's model of the user's model is compatible with our approach of considering interactions between the perspectives of the actors; thinking in terms of the way the designer perceives the user is similar in many ways to thinking about the link from the perspective of the designer to the perspective of the user. In our case the user can be thought of as being either the teacher or the student, and in some ways it is helpful to think of the links from designer to student and to teacher as expressions of the designer's models of, respectively, the student's model and the teacher's model. Thus the designer-student link is concerned with ideas about how students relate to and use software, typically raising issues concerned with cognitive development and human-computer interaction. The designer-teacher link is concerned with curriculum and associated pedagogies, typically raising issues of curriculum development and approaches to teaching.

Definitions for the Paradigm

Before discussing in more detail the three interactions in our paradigm we shall clarify what we mean by the individual perspectives of the student, the teacher and the designer.

By the *student* we mean the person or persons whose learning is to be in some way facilitated or enhanced by interaction with the environment in which the software is used. Students of a wide range of ages, abilities, motivations and interests use educational software, and when computer-assisted learning activities are designed and used, account must be taken of the particular needs of different types of students. However, it is also possible to consider the ways in which students use software in more general functional terms. This way of thinking, about the general or typical student, is used by software designers in planning learner interfaces and other features of programs. It must also, to some extent, be used by teachers in selecting computer-based learning materials for student use. The student perspective in our paradigm, then, should be understood in this latter sense.

The *teacher* in our framework is the person who guides, in whatever way and to whatever extent, the learning taking place in a computer-assisted learning environment. This is again a general use of the term, covering a wide range of software users with different needs resulting from different amounts of experience and expertise, different subject areas and student age groups, and so on. As with students, although there is enormous variety among teachers and the ways in which they interact with educational software, it is possible — and often helpful — to think in a functional way about a generalized teacher in the computer-assisted learning environment.

The term *designer* is also used in a functional way in the framework. It is taken to include all of the functions associated with design of educational software, from its conception to its completion. These include devising the initial idea for a program, designing the user interface and screen displays, writing the program code, preparing the documentation, trialling and so on. In most cases these tasks would be carried out by a number of people, but, consistent with the approach taken with the other two perspectives, we use designer as a general term to cover all of these functions.

Perspectives Interactions in the Paradigm

In considering the interaction between the perspectives of the student and the teacher (we shall shorten this to student-teacher interaction), educational software can be regarded as a potential catalyst for innovative forms of classroom interactions between teachers and students. A number of writers have noted that when software is used in the classroom the nature of interactions between both teachers and students and between students themselves can change (see for example OTA, 1988), and it is possible to identify some general characteristics of the changes in the roles of both teacher and student. Often software can be used to facilitate small group work, with resulting increases in student-student discussion. Teachers can take various interesting classroom roles when software is used, and students can take more responsibility for their own learning in computer-based environments. These and other aspects of the student-teacher interaction will be discussed in Chapter 8.

The interaction between the perspectives of the designer and the student (we shall refer to this as the designer-student interaction) is essentially concerned with how students use educational software to support their learning. At one level this involves concerns with the ease of use of software, and the learning overheads associated with becoming adept in using it efficiently and effectively. However, the central concern for this interaction is a consideration of how the development of cognitive processes can be supported. This involves consideration of models of learning and how they are reflected in software design, typically involving the issue of the level of control that the student has in using the software. Both of these aspects of the designer-student interaction are discussed in detail in Chapter 9.

The interaction between the perspectives of the designer and the teacher (the designer-teacher interaction) is concerned with curriculum issues. This involves consideration of both process and content and how they relate to computer-based learning, and more specifically to software selection. These perceptions can be examined from a cross-curriculum and a subject focused point of view.

The Characteristics of the Perspectives Interactions Paradigm

The perspectives interactions paradigm differs from previous frameworks for thinking about educational software in its emphasis on interactions between the perspectives of the actors in the computer-based educational environment. This enables a more comprehensive treatment of the area, and moves the emphasis in discussion away from consideration of the (predominantly technical) attributes of educational software packages, and toward consideration of more educational issues such as learning processes, classroom activities, teacher roles, curriculum issues, student responsibility for learning, and many other related matters as we shall show in the following chapters.

A most significant value of the perspectives interactions paradigm is that it is generative. Unlike the frameworks described in Chapter 6, the perspectives paradigm provides an overall model from which issues can be developed in context. The other frameworks have as their fundamental rationale some form of classification. Using one of these frameworks the assessor of software can place a package in a 'pigeon hole': an application type, a software role, or a curriculum perspective. However, this done, it is not clear how next to move to thinking about the educational questions which are important. The perspectives paradigm does not classify software at all. By considering the interactions between the perspectives of the designer, teacher and student, the assessor adopts a comprehensive view of the design and use of the educational software, and identifies issues that are of significance in the context of the perceived use of the software being assessed.

8 The Teacher and Student Perspectives Interaction

This chapter and the two that follow examine the three perspectives interactions described in the framework outlined in Chapter 7. Chapter 9 looks at the designer and student perspectives interaction and Chapter 10 at the designer and teacher perspectives interaction. In this chapter we examine issues arising from consideration of the teacher and student perspectives interaction part of the paradigm.

On many occasions when software is used much of the learning occurs through activities involving social interactions in the classroom, these activities being initiated or sponsored by the software. We focus here on interactions between students and teachers, or among students, rather than direct interactions between individual learners working with the software at the computer. We are particularly interested in the potential of software packages to engender valuable learning experiences through providing a stimulus for such activities. Some of these will occur as pairs or groups of students work at machines, and many may be undertaken away from the machine in the wider classroom environment.

It has been found that as a result of many of the activities enabled when software is used, students can take greater responsibility for their own learning than is otherwise the case. This has implications for teacher roles in classrooms where software is used, and for various aspects of classroom climate such as student motivation. These issues will be examined in the following sections. Then the chapter considers the implications for software selection of these issues.

Classroom Activities

There is almost no limit to the variety of worthwhile off-computer activities that might be stimulated or focused by educational software packages. For example we saw in the case of *Flowers of Crystal*, described in Chapter 4, that one primary class working in groups with a single microcomputer based a six-week unit completely around the program, including activities in art and craft, drama and movement, mathematics, science, geography, social studies, and language development.

Lewis (1986) lists a number of common classroom learning activities:

— listening (and perhaps thinking);
— listening and writing;
— listening and drawing;
— listening, seeing and analyzing;
— reading and doing;
— listening and talking;
— seeing, listening and building;
— talking and thinking;
— doing and talking;
— and so on.

(Lewis, 1986 p. 2)

These provide a starting point for thinking about activities that might be sponsored by software designed for the purpose, or software-related activities that might be devised by teachers.

Some software packages are deliberately designed to sponsor off-computer activities such as class discussion, small group research projects, and so on. This may be done by inclusion in the package of print or other materials for use in class. One example is the *First Fleet Convicts* package (Wills, 1986), a database containing information about the convicts on the First Fleet ships from England to Australia, which is accompanied by maps, a story booklet, and worksheets to be used in a range of off-computer enquiry learning activities. Alternatively, the teacher support materials with a package might simply suggest activities for the class as a whole, to be carried out in connection with the package. For example, the Teacher's Guide provided with *Factory* (Kosel and Fish, 1983), a program to develop problem solving skills, suggests that teachers '. . . brainstorm with the class on when you use the skill of working backwards to solve a problem' (Kosel and Fish, 1983 p. 10).

Some packages include printed, audio, audiovisual or other materials to be used by students in conjunction with the software for reading, writing, research and many other types of classroom activities; some provide a focus for small group discussion, cooperation, planning, record keeping and problem solving at the computer; others clearly indicate data collection and classification or similar activities as prerequisite to or part of their use.

Other packages, although not deliberately designed in this way, can nevertheless be used by teachers to provide stimulus or support for off-computer classroom activities which are valuable for learning. For example drill exercises in spelling might be exploited to encourage students to use dictionaries.

Rajaratnam (1988) illustrates a range of learning activities observed when children were using a program called *Write*; note how many of these are the result of students interacting with each other and with the teacher, in addition to those resulting from direct interaction with the computer.

While using the WRITE program:

1   The children were verbalizing and constructively discussing their story.
2   They were gaining from each other's strength in spelling, reading, vocabulary, imagination and experience.
3   They were learning to draft, edit and punctuate.
4   They were learning to associate capital letters with their lower case alphabets.
5   They were progressing with their reading as they worked through their story.
6   They were encouraged to learn to read, so that they would be able to read to their colleagues and to their parents.
7   Children with poor hand co-ordination and illegible handwriting were encouraged to write long stories. They had no fear of messy work.
8   They had no worry about making mistakes, since there was no evidence left once the work was edited, and they were gaining confidence.
9   Clearness of text made it easy for others to read. There was no drudgery of copying it out neatly for class display. It was all done by the computer.
10   Children were able to concentrate for a much longer period and produced better results.

(Rajaratnam, 1988 p. 46)

Similarly the survey by the United States Office of Technology Assessment found a variety of valuable off-computer classroom activities being sponsored by software.

For example, teachers using the popular simulation *The Oregon Trail,* which puts students into the role of early pioneers, have incorporated subject areas beyond social studies: language arts (having students keep journals); mathematics (in planning purchases for the trip); art (making maps and drawings for the walls illustrating the journey); science (learning about climate, wildlife, and nutrition during the trip), and music (singing songs of the pioneer days). (OTA, 1988 p. 95)

Software use which stimulates student and teacher discussion and questioning is reported by many writers (see for example Chatterton, 1985; O'Shea, 1988; Hoyles, Healy and Sutherland, 1991), and typified in this statement by Reid.

> CAL lessons induce (or result in) more individual/group work, more freedom for the teacher to discuss rather than instruct, greater depth of demand and open questioning, more task oriented pupil-pupil discussion, more vocalization and development and testing of hypotheses. (Reid, 1985 p. 188)

Chatterton indicates a qualitative change in the student discussion sponsored when software is used in science practical work.

> Differences are also apparent between the pupil-pupil dialogue occurring in CAL sessions and that in practical sessions. In 'practical' work the pupils tend to concentrate on the details of the experiment, with remarks such as 'What temperature do we use?' 'How much do we add?' or 'Stir it up' far outnumbering questions about the causes of the changes observed or the reasons for a particular procedure. While the simple type of dialogue is also present when CAL is used, there is an increased tendency to discuss such things as 'What happens if we increase the temperature?' or 'Why has the yield gone down?'. The pupils are led to question the reasons behind the 'facts' generated by the computer model and to develop a 'feel' for the principles involved. (Chatterton, 1985 pp. 91–2.)

The examples of activities involving teacher-student and student-student interactions given in this section cannot be exhaustive. However, they serve to illustrate the point that software can sponsor, either explicitly in the design or by teachers' devising, many activities in addition to those involving individual student interaction with the machine. These activities, involving social interactions between teacher and students or among the students, can provide valuable opportunities for learning. In some cases activities that already take place in a classroom are enhanced by the use of software; in others the activities are qualitatively different from those that take place in the absence of computer use.

Students Working in Groups

The amount of student discussion taking place in a computer-based learning environment can be significantly affected by the number of students working at a computer. The trend, particularly since the introduction of portable computers in classrooms (NCET, 1992a), is to regard as ideal the situation where students have their own individual computers. However, Stake (1991), describing a teacher working with mathematics drill and games programs from the *PLATO* system, reports almost no student-student interaction occurring as students worked at computers on their own. When the teacher arranged for students to work in pairs she observed that 'the children helped each other and learned from each other' (Stake, 1991 p. 67).

The report from the USA Office of Technology Assessment implies that student group work is not an ideal arrangement, being 'required' as a result of limited availability of hardware. Nevertheless, the report does acknowledge the value of the cooperative learning that can result.

> Many teachers have found that having only one or a few computers in the classroom requires students to work together. This stimulates cooperative learning and peer teaching among students, and develops their communication and social skills. Even simple drill and practise programs may be used with pairs or triads of students at one terminal taking turns and helping each other. (OTA, 1988 p. 93)

Groups of two or more students might work together either at the computer itself or on activites stimulated by the software but carried out elsewhere. A good example of this is the program *Motorway Route* (Squires and Watson, 1983) which is designed specifically to promote group decision-making and class discussion of issues raised by the environmental impact of motorway construction and use.

> Experience has shown that some of the most effective uses of a microcomputer are based on work with groups of students.

Using a microcomputer in this way encourages students to talk to each other and their teacher about their problems and ideas in a very articulate and positive manner. This is in sharp contrast to many 'conventional' lessons where most of the talking is done by the teacher, with little apparent opportunity for the students to express their own ideas. (Squires, 1985 p. 66)

Many teachers (see for example Chatterton, 1985; Watson, 1993) value establishing small groups of students to work together on software-related projects and activities, to foster social skills such as collaboration, group planning, systematic recording and explanatory skills (Lewis, 1986). The following are typical observations.

The children worked in groups on DART for just over 10 days. They all had several goes and seemed to learn not only from their own experiences but also from those of others. This interaction and development of social skills in the group situation has greatly improved and enhanced the atmosphere with regards to the children. (O'Shea, 1988 p. 50)

Some programs were a useful focus for collaborative and group work activities and contributed to the development of a range of related process skills. DEVELOPING TRAY for instance, contributed to a range of speaking, listening, writing and reading skills. (Watson *et al.*, 1993 p. 94)

Chatterton notes that much of the valuable learning takes place in group interactions away from the computer itself, and emphasizes the importance of these activities when software is used, in contrast to usual practice in 'normal' lessons.

The pupil-pupil dialogue which occurs when a small group of pupils are using a CAL unit is not limited to the time spent at the keyboard but can also occur during the 'data preparation' stage and during the analysis of the results. This type of dialogue is seen as particularly beneficial when the pupils are encouraged to generate and test their own hypotheses and when they are encouraged to 'explain' their ideas to each other. 'Pupil talk' forms only a very small part of a 'normal' lesson, and an increase in this area may prove an educationally important change in lesson structure. (Chatterton, 1985 pp. 92–3)

It is evident that the interactions taking place within student groups can vary in effectiveness, and may be more valuable for some members of a group than others. Although a comprehensive examination of student group dynamics is beyond the scope of this book, we do suggest that teachers with some experience of student group work should try to anticipate the nature of likely group dynamics when a particular software environment is being assessed. For example, the British ImpacT study (Watson *et al.*, 1993) distinguished between collaboration and cooperation among students in groups using software. In some of the classes observed, pupils sitting together were not actually working together; one pupil was doing the work which was then used by another, or students took turns to work individually to generate graphs or text at the keyboard. 'Working together at a computer did not necessarily ensure collaboration. When using certain software, for example spreadsheets and word processing, pupils would take turns or share tasks rather than attempt to work together' (Watson *et al.*, 1993 p. 94).

Small group work is of course only one of a number of ways in which software can be used to sponsor activities involving teacher-student and student-student interactions for learning. It is however widely used, and does provide a helpful way to examine issues concerning classroom interactions more generally. Some of these isssues, movement of the locus of responsibility in learning activities, roles for teachers when software is used, and effects on classroom climate and organization, are explored in the following sections.

Responsibility for Learning

It is evident from classroom observations that the use of software, particularly though not only when students work in small groups, can provide an opportunity for students to take a greater responsibility for their activities and for their learning.

> The direct level of teacher involvement in the running of the software was less than in their 'normal' class. . . . There was also less teacher direction about the routes for action and all teachers encouraged the pupils to get on and decide for themselves. As the lesson progressed and points were either raised by pupils or from the teacher noticing something, teachers would then give some hints or directions or ask them to remember a relevant factor. Teachers expressed getting the pupils to make decisions and answer questions as one of the main aims for

using software. The researcher saw some impressive teaching based on carefully directed support for the pupils' exploration and learning during these sessions. (Watson *et al.*, 1993 p. 79)

Teachers who use the computer as a medium that students can manipulate individually or in small groups find their students become more actively engaged in learning and thinking than during traditional lecture-oriented lessons. Such teachers use the computers to give students more responsibility for their own learning. Students can work at their own speed and can figure out more for themselves. (OTA, 1988 pp. 91–2)

In general I was impressed with the way they tackled problems, often in a logical manner. They kept to the task in hand even when completely unsupervised. They remained enthusiastic even when faced with frustrating problems. They cooperated with each other and had an 'open' approach to the task in that they utilized each other's suggestions and were willing to challenge and ask each other for explanations. (Marchant, 1988 pp. 247–8)

A particularly exciting account of students taking responsibility for their learning and determining the directions for their study comes from an account of a class using *The Geometric Supposer* (Schwartz, Yerushalmy and Gordon, 1985), an open-ended program for investigating geometry. A case-study classroom teacher cited in the documentation accompanying the program reports:

Students worked independently on these problems both during and outside class time and occasionally asked me for hints or to clarify problem statements. When students found that they could not draw any conclusions regarding a given problem, they would group together to discuss it. These conversations often resulted in a restatement of the problem and the students went back to work on it again. . . . In fact I found some of the best problems for the course while listening to these conversations or trying to answer their questions in class. . . . For students, this means greater responsibility since the course of learning relies heavily on the findings of students and the reactions of their classmates. For teachers, this may require some flexibility and patience in their efforts to provoke and to guide productive exploration. (Schwartz, Yerushalmy, and Gordon, 1985 pp. 83–4)

Increased student autonomy in learning does not necessarily happen just because software is used. Stake (1991), describing a classroom in which software for studying graphs, whole numbers, and fractions was being used reports that the teacher '. . . organized lessons and activities so that the children had limited freedom of movement and socialization. . . . Usually they were not responsible for determining the content of their lessons. They could select when they wished to work on required lessons' (Stake, 1991 p. 57).

This transfer of responsibility, or increased student autonomy in learning, raises immediately non-trivial problems concerning teacher interventions in the student-student interactions. Teachers are trained and expert in helping students to achieve success, and in protecting them from frustration and errors. It is very difficult for people with this training to stand back and refrain from interventions when students seem puzzled or frustrated. However, while such interventions might assist students to find answers in the short term, they can also interfere with the students' taking responsibility for the learning associated with the activity being undertaken, and a careful balance must be sought. This issue is addressed at some length elsewhere (McDougall, 1988), and is illustrated by the following classroom accounts which describe students using the packages *L* and *DEVELOPING TRAY*.

> I think that one of the main strengths of *L* is the way children take such an active role and are in control, in contrast to when the teacher dominates the learning context. I listened with dismay to a tape recording of me intervening when the group were faced with a problem. The recording showed how I hurried them through to a conclusion, giving them little time to explore the problem fully and interpret it in their own way. I am not suggesting that children working in groups can be just left to get on with it, but it requires careful judgment to decide how and when to get involved so the initiative is not taken out of their hands. (Marchant, 1988 p. 247)

> I feel that I must mention the role that I played. . . . Having given the children the instructions necessary to operate the program, I was under the impression that I had left the children without too many interventions. However, upon listening to the tape, I realized just how many comments I had made. Although some of these were words of encouragement and praise, I had to admit rather humbly, that the children were far more self-sufficient than I had given them credit for, and that the majority

of my talk was superfluous! It seemed that I had underestimated their capacity for problem solving, and wonder now if they could have tackled a more difficult text in the first place. This is something that I intend to find out in my next session with them on DEVTRAY! (Poole, 1988 p. 176)

Despite this problem of gauging appropriate times and types of teacher interventions when students work autonomously, it is generally agreed that this transfer to students of a good deal of the responsibility for their learning activities is a valuable change in classroom practice and one which can be facilitated considerably by the use of suitable software.

Teacher Roles

It is now clear that the use of educational software in ways that exploit the learning potential of teacher-student and student-student interactions can have significant implications for roles for teachers in classrooms (Bishop, 1993). And indeed changes in teacher roles, associated with software use, have been reported (Chatterton, 1985; OTA, 1988; Watson *et al.*, 1993). We show here two typical accounts.

One of the most significant impacts of the use of computers in the classroom is change in teaching style. Teachers can go beyond the traditional information delivery mode whereby they are presenters of ready-made knowledge and become facilitators of students' learning. With computers, students can work on problems individually or in small groups while the teacher acts more like a coach circulating among them and giving assistance. Some teachers find that they are able to observe more of the learning process when watching students interact with computer-based materials. Some teachers welcome the opportunity to learn alongside their students. . . . For many, this is a significant change from how they were taught to teach. It can be both exhilarating and intimidating. (OTA, 1988 p. 91)

. . . the computer can relieve the teacher of the role of task-setter and allow him/her to move around the class in a supportive role — giving advice and help, prompting new ideas and checking the understanding of established concepts. (Chatterton, 1985 pp. 89–90)

Teacher as Resource Provider

To make the most of the potential of a software package to support classroom interaction activities away from the computer, the teacher's role as 'resource provider' becomes very important, as the teacher needs to collect and prepare various resources and materials for the off-computer activities. In some cases at least some of these materials will be provided as part of the printed or other support materials in the software package. In many other cases the materials supplied may need modification to suit the particular class under consideration or the specific purposes of a teacher at the time or suitable materials for the activities planned by the teacher may not be provided at all.

Other materials may need to be found, or perhaps made, for class use. Many programs can be well supported by other media resources. For example *Flowers of Crystal* (Matson, 1984), described in Chapter 4, is accompanied by a scene-setting audio tape; *Motorway Route* (Squires and Watson, 1983) mentioned earlier can be accompanied by a videotape and might be supported by use of overhead projector transparencies and a range of other materials. Resources for use with software might include videotapes, slides, pictures, posters or maps related to the topic being studied, reference books or other documents, student worksheets, materials for art, science or drama, and so on.

Teacher as Manager

The teacher's role as 'manager' in the classroom has an additional dimension when computers are used. As the OTA (1988) report points out, there are many different ways to organize use of the hardware as well as all the other resources students will use. Teachers assessing a software package need to keep this variety of management possibilities in mind as they visualize ways in which the software might be used in their classrooms.

> There are as many ways teachers can use computers in the classroom as there are varying teaching styles. Teachers use groups of computers in laboratories very differently than one or two in the classroom. A single computer in a classroom can be used by the teachers in various ways at various times — sometimes as a provocative learning station for individual students, sometimes for interactive demonstrations led by the teacher for the whole class, and in other instances for collaborative

problem solving by a small group of students. Use in social studies is different from that for science laboratory work; drill and practice for review of basic skills is very different from students programing a computer to make machines move. (OTA, 1988 p. 91)

Management of time is another matter for consideration. The class time to be allotted for using a software package in ways involving teacher-student and student-student classroom interactions will always be considerably more than the time taken to run the program in isolation. Since much of the learning will take place in class discussions, student recording, small group planning or similar activities, plenty of time must be allowed for these. It might take just a short browsing time for a teacher to investigate how a program runs, but the actual class time needed for students to carry out the activities that make using the program worthwhile might be several lessons or more and could be very difficult to predict.

Teacher as Coach

Chatterton (1985) and the US Office of Technology Assessment (1988) both report teachers, in classrooms in which software was providing a focus for activities, acting in a role they refer to as 'coach'. Chatterton's description, for example, provides a useful account of the actual activities being undertaken by the teachers and students in this case.

> The nature of the episodes themselves is also changed: for example, the number of teacher-based 'explaining' and 'initiating' episodes is reduced, while the number of episodes of 'coaching' (teacher working with an individual or small group of pupils) and, within a group of pupils, of 'arguing' or 'searching' (for a pattern or answer) is increased. Indeed, the SCAN records show that, for small-group work activities in lessons involving CAL, 'coaching' forms the basis of the great majority of teacher-initiated episodes. (Chatterton, 1985 p. 91)

Teacher as Researcher

The possibility that use of educational software might reveal information about learning processes is regarded as most important in research work (see for example Weir, 1987). At the classroom level it appears that the 'mind mirroring' characteristics of software use can provide teachers with insights about learning processes and difficulties of their students, suggesting a role for the teacher as 'researcher'.

> From the observations of children using *DEVELOPING TRAY*... it became clear that the program had potential as a diagnostic tool, which could provide more complex information about children's reading skills than the standardized reading tests being used by the school. (Watson *et al.*, 1993 p. 76)

Teacher as Facilitator

These somewhat newer roles for teachers, when software is used, should not detract from the teacher's fundamental responsibility as 'facilitator' of students' learning, and, as the following illustration indicates, thought must be given to preparing students adequately for making the most of the potential of the software packages that are being used.

> Then I used *INDIAN FARMER* as an experiment and the children went absolutely wild.... This is a program where you have people dying, build up families. What was worrying, I couldn't get them off the machine, there was long laughter, the more people died the more laughter there was, and I almost felt I would have serious reservations about doing it again despite the fact that it actually captured them ... because I have great suspicions that it didn't actually capture them for the right reasons. They weren't horrified with what was happening, they found it amusing. (Classroom teacher quoted in Watson *et al.*, 1993 pp. 81–2)

This overview of teacher roles shows that the roles available to teachers working in classrooms where software is used are very varied. However, decisions by teachers in this context are critically important if software is to be used effectively to enhance student learning.

Classroom Interaction Issues in Software Selection

A one-off assessment of a software package as 'good' or 'poor' or a review rating of '8 out of 10', is, in the context of thinking about the interactions of the perspectives of the teacher and the student, essentially meaningless. A program that seems technically relatively trivial or otherwise uninspiring might, when used in a particular way, become part of a very significant classroom learning environment (Preece and Jones, 1985) or provide a personal learning experience which is well suited to a student with particular needs. Just one example is a program called *Counter* (Wigley, 1985) which simply shows a sequence of counting numbers, one at a time, on the screen. At first this program seems too simple to be of any use at all; however materials accompanying the program and accounts of its use in several classroom situations (Waddington and Wigley, 1985; Aston, 1990) make it evident that in the hands of a well prepared or inventive teacher this program can provide a focus for some fascinating and worthwhile problem-solving activities in various areas of algebra and number theory.

A number of writers support this view of the importance of classroom interactions and teacher roles when software is used, and the lack of value in one-off assessments of educational software packages. We provide here two examples.

> The view expressed . . . was that neither software reviews nor software evaluations are important since it is how the teacher uses the software in the classroom that counts. In order to come to a better understanding of the computer's impact on learning, there is a need for classroom observations of effective uses of software integrated into the curriculum. There is consequently no *good* or *bad* software. Some uses are effective and others are inappropriate; some teachers are clever and others are not so clever; some environments are favourable and others are not. (OECD, 1989 pp. 106–7)

> Good software can be used inappropriately and bad software can achieve merits not hitherto seen in skilful hands. The worthwhileness of the software is also dependent on the particular setting in which it is used and the approach of the learners as well as the teachers. (Watson *et al.*, 1993 p. 82)

Related to the interaction of the perspectives of the teacher and the student, there are many questions teachers might have in mind as they examine educational software packages to make selection decisions. At the most general level, a useful question would concern the kinds of classroom activities and interactions that might be sponsored by a package. More specific questions would consider the organization of computer use in the classroom, possible interactions associated with student group work and whole-class discussion, the relationship between computer-based and off-computer activities, the extent to which students might take responsibility for their activities and their learning in using the package, the amount and nature of teacher intervention that might be appropriate, teacher roles and styles of classroom management that might facilitate learning with the package, and the suitability of all of these for the classroom setting in which the software is to be used.

The potential for software use to enable students to take a larger amount of responsibility for their learning, and the complexity of roles for teachers implied by this, enables teachers to think in terms of a great variety of possible classroom interactions and classroom climates as they plan software based learning experiences for their students. The software selection issues here are much more complex than can be addressed in checklists of software attributes, such as those shown in Chapter 3.

9 The Designer and Student Perspectives Interaction

Perhaps the most important consideration in assessing educational software is the way in which it can be used to enhance students' learning. If a package does not in some way support or enhance learning, it is obviously of little educational value. The theory of learning that the designer has adopted as a basis for development of software is a critical aspect of software assessment. The views about learning underlying the design define the essential character of the interaction between the perspectives of the designer and the student; software developed by a 'behaviourist' designer will have a very different character from software designed by a 'Piagetian' designer. A major concern in software selection is to identify the theory of learning underpinning the package, and to decide whether this theory is appropriate for the intended educational tasks.

An associated critical aspect of assessment in this context is the effectiveness of the software design in realizing the consequences of the adopted theory. The designer may have laudable and innovative ideas, but unless the software is 'accessible' and easy to use these ideas will count for little. Considering accessibility in selecting software can be thought of as an exercise in assessing the quality of the user interface. However, care should be taken not to put undue emphasis on cosmetic design features at the expense of more fundamental aspects of human-computer interaction. A more insightful approach is required to assess the significant features of the designer-student interaction. In the following section we develop such an approach.

Learning Issues in Software Design

A crude distinction can be drawn between two opposing theories of learning which have been very influential in the design of educational software. One view, originating from the behaviourist school of psychology, regards learning in terms of a stimulus-response mechanism. Learning is thought to take place in the following way: the learner is presented with some material to which they are expected to make a response; based on this response the teacher (or a delegated authority such as a programmed learning text) provides feedback. Positive feedback encourages the learner to internalize the 'lesson' and negative feedback prompts the student to 'think again'. Perhaps the best known exponent of this view of learning is Skinner (see Skinner, 1938 for a full treatment of this approach).

The opposing view, originating from the constructivist school of psychology, regards learning as a process of accommodation and assimilation in which learners modify their internal cognitive structures through experience. Learning is considered to be a personal and idiosyncratic experiential process which the teacher facilitates by organizing and supporting appropriate learning environments. Piaget is the classic exponent of this view of learning. These two extreme caricatures of learning theories are crude stereotypes, and there are a range of theories and views about learning which fall between. Nevertheless, we shall use these two stereotypes to illustrate the essential features of learning theories that are used as the basis for software design.

There is obviously a marked difference between the behaviourist approach and the constructivist approach. Behaviourists consider learners to be passive individuals who can be 'spoon fed' knowledge in a way that is independent of their own cognitive state. On the other hand, constructivists consider learners to be active participants in the process, learning in a way that depends on their current cognitive state. These radically different perceptions of the learner are manifested in the design of learning materials. Behaviourist learning materials provide fixed instructional sequences, with each step in the sequence based on the acquisition of a limited piece of knowledge and understanding. Computer-based drills are the classic manifestation of the behaviourist approach to educational software design (for a justification of this approach see Suppes, 1967). A common claim for these drills is that extensive carefully structured practice leads to the effective and efficient development of basic skills, allowing learners to concentrate on higher level cognition. Constructivist materials emphasize personal expression and exploration, with opportunities for students to pursue their own approaches to learning. The advocates of computer-based microworlds are vociferous in their claims that using educational software should be a constructivist activity. Papert epitomizes their case:

Briefly, a microworld is a subset of reality or constructed reality whose structure matches that of a given cognitive mechanism so as to provide an environment where the latter can operate effectively. The concept leads to the project of inventing microworlds so structured as to allow a human learner to exercise particular powerful ideas or intellectual skills. (Papert, 1980a p. 204)

Papert maintains that the advent of microcomputers has made the use of these microworlds a real possibility. The consequent claims for the use of microworlds have often been radical and fundamental. For example, there are research based claims that progression through Piaget's stages of development can be accelerated through the use of microworlds (see for example Lawler, 1985; McDougall, 1990).

In some cases the learning theory underpinning a package is made explicit, making assessment in this respect relatively straightforward. At best the learning theory is clearly stated in documentation accompanying the package, or there may be a more general statement in the literature about the theories underpinning a particular approach to software design. In other cases the theory is implicit, and an important part of assessment is to identify the 'hidden' theory of learning. This is a matter of interpretation, and brings some uncertainty to the assessment process. In some cases an underpinning learning theory may be absent, and this is indicative of software likely to have little or no value in educational settings. It may seem quite incredible that such 'vacuous' material exists, but unfortunately it is not uncommon. Sewell makes this point with reference to some software allegedly based on the behaviourist approach:

Some so-called educational software which provides more interesting and exciting screen displays when an incorrect answer is given reveal a disturbing lack of awareness of the theoretical origins of the behaviourist approach they are, unconsciously adopting. With such programs, the danger is that the child who is prone to error receives little, if any, remedial help, and may come to associate the intrinsically more interesting sequence of events with particular erroneous responses, a situation completely at variance with the original formulation of operant conditioning (Sewell, 1990 p. 65)

Learning Issues in Software Assessment

The frequently implicit nature of learning theories used in software design makes their assessment very difficult. However, it is essential that this assessment is made for two reasons:

(i)   to decide whether the learning theories are appropriate to the selector's perceived approaches to teaching and learning;

(ii)   to judge whether the software design is consistent with the approach to learning in the classroom environment that the software is intended to support.

To assist with this it is possible to devise an assessment heuristic which can be used in the identification of these learning theories. These heuristics are based on three aspects of software design: the extent of *learner control*, the *complexity* of the material presented to learners; and the *challenge* felt by learners. The notion of learner control as a significant descriptor of computer-based learning is well established. For example it features in the frameworks proposed by Wellington (1985) and Chandler (1984) as an organizing theme for software classification (see Chapter 6). McDougall and Squires (1986) postulate learner control as a method and Blease (1986) refers to its use in discussing frameworks for the classification of educational software. The work of Malone (1981) highlights the motivating power of challenging computer-based environments. Complexity concerns both the content and the processes supported by the software, and as such has a clear relationship with the adopted theory of learning.

The designer-student interaction can be viewed in terms of each of these aspects to provide a heuristic for software assessment. The learning theory underpinning the software is in large part characterized by the extent to which the designer has delegated control to the learner, the scope of the complexity that the designer has defined, and the nature of the challenges which the designer has incorporated. These can be related to learning theories to develop an assessment heuristic as shown in Figure 9.1.

Research by Wishart (1989) indicates that increasing learner control is most significant in enhancing learning. A combination of challenge and complexity with learner control appears to be even more effective. Combining control and complexity seems to develop a feeling of involvement, but combining control and challenge is more effective in promoting learning. These findings suggest that a consideration of learner control should form the focus in assessment, though complexity and challenge also warrant attention. More specifically this approach leads to four important general questions:

(i)   What are the levels of learner control, task complexity, and challenge offered by the package?

	Behaviourism	**Constructivism**
Learner control	Little or no control with learners regarded as passive consumers	Significant levels of control with learners regarded as active, purposeful participants
Complexity	Highly structured material presented in simple formats, with small steps to maximize the chance of positive feedback.	Material which is typically complex, allowing a variety of content to be considered and a range of processes to be exercised
Challenge	Artificially contrived rewards, typically taking the form of unrelated extrinsic rewards such as the presentation of attractive illustrations or the use of sound.	Intrinsic rewards gained by the successful completion of complex tasks.

Figure 9.1   An assessment heuristic for learning issues

(ii)   How effective is the design in affording learners the intended level of control?

(iii)   How are learners helped to cope with the complexity of the software?

(iv)   What methods and approaches are used to provide learners with a challenge?

It must be stressed that this assessment heuristic is only intended as a guide. Adopted learning theories will typically not fit into the simplistic division between behaviourism and constructivism. Assessors should be beware of classifying software as either 'constructivist' (and, given current fashions, by implication a good package) or 'behaviourist'. Recently developed educational software may adopt two approaches to learning in parallel — witness the current trend to develop exploratory based learning packages (Cox and Cumming, 1990) in which tutorial modules are linked to microworlds, as in *Smithtown*, described by its designers as an 'intelligent discovery world' (Shute and Glaser, 1990).

In the next section we shall describe some examples of educational software packages to illustrate use of the assessment heuristic. The examples are all chosen from the same subject area, transformation geometry, and, given the importance of learner control, they are presented in order of increasing learner control.

Illustration of an Assessment Heuristic: Some Examples

The learning of transformation geometry is an area that has well documented pedagogical and conceptual difficulties associated with it. Many of these are concerned with logical deduction and with the visualization and manipulation of spatial problems, and it is reasonable to expect that software using computer graphics might help overcome many of these difficulties. First, we consider a computer-based drill in geometry topics. Next is a simulation of processes in the production of punched and painted objects, aiming to provide students with an opportunity to solve problems in simple transformation geometry. Then we discuss two interactive graphics packages, one designed to represent basic geometrical transformations and the other concerned with the geometry of triangles. The last example is a *Logo* geometry microworld.

Computer-Based Geometry Drill Programs

There are many drill programs designed for students to practise skills related to geometry topics (see, for example, Straker, 1990). We shall consider a hypothetical example representative of the typical features of these programs, a drill providing an elementary introduction to the measurement of angles. Students are presented with a series of diagrams and requested to enter a value for the currently depicted angle. They are informed whether their estimate is correct (within specified margins of error) and a score of correct responses is kept.

Learner control in this hypothetical example is virtually nonexistent. The designer has exercised maximum power in prescribing the nature of the learner's interaction with the software. Learners control only the pace at which they answer the drill questions, and ultimately the decision to walk away from the computer when they get bored. The relationship between accessibility and control in this example is essentially unimportant. Similarly the issue of complexity is largely irrelevant in this context; the drill simply presents learners with sequences of questions. In more sophisticated branching programs there may be a limited element of choice about what to do next, but as a matter of principle 'behaviourist' designers strive to make each step in the use of a program non-problematic; the smaller the step the more likely the learner is to make it correctly.

In contrast to learner control and complexity, the issue of challenge is highly relevant in assessing computer-based drills. Reward for successful completion of prescribed tasks is an essential feature of a behaviourist approach, and most computer-based drills incorporate challenge through some form of reward mechanism. The most common way of providing this is to give a score of correct answers; a feature of our hypothetical angles drill. There is clearly a link between this form of reward and a learner's progress. Links with other common reward mechanisms can be more tenuous. Animated colourful displays and sound can be used to provide reward, but their use is often unconnected with the subject matter of the drill and can provide a distraction rather than a challenge. A drill for infant pupils in which the successful completion of arithmetic problems is rewarded by computer generated nursery rhymes would be typical of this approach. In some cases the links between displays and sound are designed to relate to the subject being drilled.

Thinking about learner control, complexity and challenge allows the essential educational characteristics of the angles drill to be assessed. The virtual absence of learner control, a lack of complexity, and the use of contrived challenges clearly indicate a behaviourist learning model. Of these three issues, in this case challenge is the only one providing a range of apposite assessment questions. How effective is the reward mechanism? Is the reward mechanism consistent with the subject being drilled, or is it simply an attractive diversion?

Using this heuristic to identify learning theories is not necessarily a judgmental activity; rather it is a means by which learning theories implicit in software can be matched against perceived educational needs. Underwood and Underwood (1990) point out, with reference to the use of drills to develop skills in word recognition and spelling: 'The practice of such skills is not inherently wrong — indeed practice is vital if skills are to reach the level of automaticity necessary to allow the individual to focus attention on higher-level problems' (Underwood and Underwood, 1990 p. 22).

If the aim is to select software which will foster automaticity in the estimation of angles, while essential concepts and ideas are to be presented in other ways, this hypothetical example may be an appropriate choice. If software is being sought which will encourage children to explore ideas and concepts associated with angles in personally significant ways this software is obviously an inappropriate choice.

A Problem-Solving Package Involving Spatial Skills: 'Factory'

Whilst *Factory* (Kosel and Fish, 1983) is not specifically intended to teach transformation geometry, rotation is one of the processes that students can investigate when they use the software. The program enables students to specify three simple operations that can be performed on a square object: painting stripes of three different thicknesses, punching square or circular holes, and rotating through one of four angles. Three parts to the program enable students to 'test a machine', 'build a factory', and 'make a product'. To test a machine students specify an operation, such as punching two circular holes, and see its effect. This part of the program enables students to become familiar with the basic operations of the factory's machines. Building a factory consists of defining operations for each of up to eight sequentially ordered machines. The result of these operations on a square object will then be displayed on the screen. Making a product sets production problems. Students are shown a square object which has experienced a number of operations, and requested to specify a sequence of machines to produce such an object. After the sequence has been specified the square will be processed to see whether students have 'worked back' correctly to identify a correct sequence.

Learners have some autonomy when they use *Factory*; in building a factory students control the assembly line sequence, and in making a product students have a similar level of control in working backwards to specify a sequence to produce a defined product. It is clear that students are expected to learn through exploration, using their control over the software in the building a factory section to experiment with sequencing. Similarly, the making a product section provides an opportunity for students to use this control so as to try other cognitive control strategies, such as process analysis and working backwards. No extrinsic rewards are provided in *Factory*; the successful completion of tasks, either originating from the learner in the building a factory section or from the designer in the making a product section, is intended to provide a sufficient implicit challenge. The complexity is limited; only three different types of operation are possible, and very restricted ranges of inputs are allowed for these operations. It appears that the designer has made the conscious decision to restrict the complexity of the learning environment; possibly in an attempt to focus on specific problem-solving skills rather than content: 'The Factory is designed to teach . . . Strategies. It focuses on several [. . .] strategies: working backwards, analyzing a process, determining a sequence and applying creativity' (Kosel and Fish, 1984 p. 1).

In this case possible advantages of complexity have been sacrificed in order to concentrate on well-defined process skills. This may be valuable in achieving these restricted aims, but the approach limits the extent to which *Factory* can be used, probably restricting its value to use on a single occasion.

Using our assessment heuristic indicates an implicit theory of learning which is compatible with a constructivist approach; learners have significant control over the operation of the program, and the problem-solving context provided by the program is challenging and motivating in its own right. However, thinking about complexity raises some interesting issues about the extent to which this theory of learning has been adopted. The designer has assumed that specific problem-solving skills are best learned in relatively simple environments. This could be construed as contrary to a fully constructivist approach in which the development of skills is seen as being enhanced by the mental struggle to assimilate complex structures. Critical aspects of assessing this program will be concerned with the validity in particular classroom settings of this limit in complexity, and whether the level of control compensates to provide sufficient opportunities for learners to express and explore their own ideas and concepts.

Geometry Packages Using Interactive Graphics: 'Transformations' and 'The Geometric Supposer'

Transformations (Alderson, Blakeley, Millwood and Deane, 1992) is concerned with the basic operations of transformation geometry; translation, reflection, rotation and magnification. The graphical capabilities of the computer are used to illustrate the effect of these transformations, applied either singly or in combination, on shapes that can be defined by a student. Rectilinear shapes can be drawn very easily on the screen and sequences of transformations are defined by making selections from simple menus. Students can apply sequences of transformations to test their own hypotheses. For example, is a reflection followed by a translation equivalent to a translation followed by a reflection?

The Geometric Supposer (Schwartz, Yerushalmy, and Gordon, 1985) provides an environment in which students can make conjectures about geometrical constructions associated with triangles. (There is also a version of the program which deals with quadrilaterals). Various geometrical constructions (segment, circle, median, altitude, parallel, perpendicular, angle bisector, perpendicular bisector, midsegment, extension) can be applied to a chosen triangle, and a variety of geometrical parameters can be measured (length, perimeter, area, angle, distance from a point to a line, distance from a line to another line). By applying constructions and taking measurements students are in a position to make geometrical conjectures about the properties of triangles. For example, a reasonable supposition might be that the median divides a triangle into two halves. By constructing the median and measuring areas of the two triangles so formed this supposition can be tested.

Both *The Geometric Supposer* and *Transformations* allow learners significant control. In *The Geometric Supposer* the conjecture of geometrical theorems is left totally to learners, who are able to choose constructions and measurements at will. Using *Transformations* learners can define their own shapes to investigate, and specify the transformations sequence and associated input values. As in *Factory*, challenge is regarded as being implicit in the task itself; in the case of both of these programs the task is doing innovative mathematics. In the words of the designers of *The Geometric Supposer*:

> There is something odd about the way we teach mathematics in our schools. We make little or no provision for students to play an active and generative role in learning mathematics and we teach mathematics as if we expected that students will never have occasion to invent new mathematics. . . . The central activity of creating new mathematics — the making and testing of conjectures — is absent from the classroom. . . . But with the aid of the *The Geometric Supposer* as intellectual amplifier, conjecture can assume its proper role as a key activity in the learning and teaching of geometry. (Schwartz *et al.*, 1985 p. 1)

In one sense the complexity of both packages is bounded, as they deal with well defined subsets of subject areas. However, each of these packages can support complex investigations within these subsets; the sequence of transformations can be as complicated as the learner wishes, and the conjectures can involve as many constructions and measurements as desired by the learner. Of course, learners are restricted to those transformations, constructions, and measurements provided by the packages, but quite complex investigations are possible.

Consideration of learner control, complexity and challenge indicates that both of these packages have adopted a constructivist model of learning. Learner control is high (within well defined subject boundaries), the use of each program is intended to be implicitly challenging, and there is the possibility of some complexity involving learners in setting their own learning tasks. A detailed assessment of both of

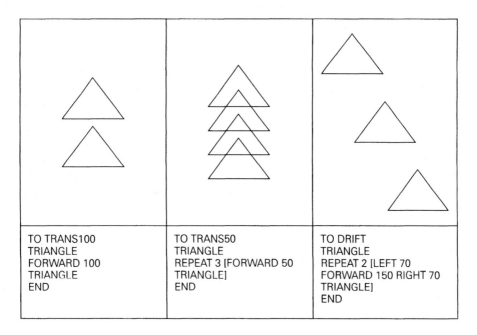

TO TRANS100	TO TRANS50	TO DRIFT
TRIANGLE	TRIANGLE	TRIANGLE
FORWARD 100	REPEAT 3 [FORWARD 50	REPEAT 2 [LEFT 70
TRIANGLE	TRIANGLE]	FORWARD 150 RIGHT 70
END	END	TRIANGLE]
		END

Figure 9.2   Translation and rotation procedures in Logo

these programs would raise questions similar to the following. Do learners have enough control to express sufficiently their intentions? How can they express this control? Given the potentially complex nature of the learning environments, can learners navigate themselves around the program without too much difficulty?

Turtle Geometry: A Microworld in 'Logo'

A transformation geometry microworld can be developed in *Logo* by writing a suite of procedures to effect translation, rotation, reflection and magnification. Some representative procedures designed to help learners explore the concepts of translation are shown in Figure 9.2.

Learners can adapt and combine procedures by writing completely new procedures. They can do essentially all the activities possible in the previously discussed software packages. However, there are radical differences in the way in which learners are able to complete these activities. Learners have much more control over the software which they can express through actual programming in *Logo*. They can define the transformations and the way that they are implemented, and they can become involved in complex environments by applying programming techniques such as recursion. As procedures are added and linked to each other the complexity will increase. The software itself offers no real direction on how to handle this complexity; there are no menus or explicit suggestions for activities. The only way to cope is by reading and manipulating the *Logo* procedures which constitute the microworld. Challenge is implicit in the task of building, extending and exploring the microworld — there are no 'bells and whistles' to reward success; exploration and discovery are intended to be rewards in themselves.

The notion of a transformation geometry microworld is clearly based on a constructivist theory of learning. While developing procedures to articulate and manipulate ideas such as rotation, magnification and so on, learners are involved in a constructive process, not unlike that of actually teaching these concepts; this must be accompanied by development of a very full understanding of the ideas. Learners are regarded as active and purposeful, with a large measure of control over the learning environment in which they are working. They are expected to find the activity challenging in its own right, and to be prepared to cope with complexity.

A fully fledged adoption of a constructivist theory of learning raises some very important assessment questions. In reality how controllable by the students is the microworld? It is all very well making a high level of learner control available, but learners must be able to exercise this control easily, without undue cognitive overheads. In the case of a *Logo* microworld the control is effected through programming, but it is well known that programming presents many learners with considerable difficulty (see for example Cope and Walsh, 1990). The programming overheads may prevent students from using the transformation microworld; they might simply be unable to cope with the programming required to enable them to extend and control the microworld. It could even be that the cognitive demands of learning to program to an adequate level are greater than the cognitive demands associated with learning transformation geometry! The ability of learners to handle very complex environments is also problematical, given that the means of dealing with this complexity is programming. The clarity and relevance of the procedures which are initially provided as a basis for the microworld development are important considerations here. How understandable are they? How easy are they to modify? How comprehensive is the microworld that they initially define?

Summary

In this chapter we have identified the learning theory adopted by the designer as being of major significance in defining the essential characteristics of the designer-student interaction. Sometimes the theory is made explicit in the accompanying documentation, but in most cases it is simply implicit in the software design, and in some cases it is even absent! A critical aspect of software selection in the context of the designer-student interaction is to identify implicit theories of learning and decide whether (i) these are appropriate to perceived needs, and (ii) the software design is consistent with the theory. We have developed and described an assessment heuristic, based on the issues of learner control, complexity, and challenge, which can be used to indicate the nature of implicit theories of learning, and to prompt questions concerned with how well the software design matches the implications of the adopted learning theory.

10 The Designer and Teacher Perspectives Interaction

The vast majority of educational software packages are used in organized contexts in which a teacher has a formal responsibility to participate in 'delivering' a curriculum. The curriculum varies widely in design and delivery from country to country, and even within countries, but in all locations teachers have this responsibility. This implies that the essential aspects of the interaction between the perspectives of the designer and the teacher are the possible relationships of the software to the curriculum. The design of the software incorporates a representation of the designer's perception of the curriculum, so assessment in the context of the designer-teacher interaction becomes a question of the extent to which the designer's perception of the curriculum matches that of the selector. However, it is not simply a case of the teacher acquiescing to the designer's curriculum imperatives; rather it is a case of interpreting how appropriate the designer's intentions are to perceived needs, and, possibly, how these intentions might be modified. Modifications can be the result of using the software in novel ways, or they may result from making changes to the software itself.

Curriculum Issues in Software Design

Although curriculum is stated and delivered in many different ways, all curricula are concerned with a definition of educational *content* and *process*. Educational software can help the effective delivery of curriculum with respect to both content and process. The storage and retrieval of information is a defining rationale for the use of computers, and curriculum content can be regarded as a particular form of information which is amenable to computer-based processing. In addition, the interactive nature of computers provides the potential for radical contributions to the support and extension of process based work.

In the design of a software package aspects of the curriculum can be explicit, either as statements in the accompanying documentation, or in terms of the subject content and the processes supported by software. However, these aspects are often implicit in the design of the software. Indeed the designer may not even realize that they are there. On occasion curriculum aspects are initially absent from the design, as is the case when software designed for use in commerce and industry is 'high-jacked' for use in education.

Educational Software and Explicit Curriculum Issues

In some packages curriculum issues are clearly stated. Some packages have been developed collaboratively with a curriculum development project, leading to very specifically articulated curriculum aims. For example, software was commissioned to form an integral part of the revised Nuffield A-level Physics course. The software consisted of a modelling package (Ogborn, 1985) and a suite of subject specific programs (Harris, 1985). These programs are referred to in the teaching materials for the course, making selection an almost trivial matter.

Other software has been deliberately designed to support the existing curriculum. *Nuclides Database* (Bennett, 1987), a simple database program which allows students to obtain information on a large number of nuclides, is intended to support a nuclear physics option in the Joint Matriculation Board A-Level physics course:

> Students following the Joint Matriculation Board (JMB) nuclear physics option at Advanced Level will find in the database all the information in the JMB 'Notes for Guidance'. (Bennett, 1987 p. 4)

Another example of explicit reference to the curriculum is given by Watson in describing software designed by the Computers in the Curriculum Project to accompany the Schools Council History 13–16 Project:.

> The various units focus on selected aspects of the examination course and resource material provided by the History 13–16 Project. They are designed to support the more investigative

styles of learning to which both Projects are committed. (Watson, 1986 p. 1)

Explicit articulation of the curriculum relevance of software is often given in terms of content, so it is interesting to note that Watson refers to both content and process. Occasionally, the norm is reversed, and the emphasis is placed on process. For example, *Priority* (Flavell, Gomberg, and Squires, 1993), a project management program which produces data for export to commonly available spreadsheets, is primarily intended to support the development of modelling skills:

'Priority' is an educational software package designed primarily to support the Information Technology component of the Technology National Curriculum (Attainment Target 5). In particular, it is intended to enhance the teaching of the modelling strand of AT 5. (Flavell, Gomberg, and Squires, 1993 p. 3)

However even when curriculum issues are not referred to in documentation, the content of a package is often sufficiently explicit to indicate the curriculum focus of the package. This is particularly so in subject-based packages. The more specific the subject focus is, the easier it is to identify a curriculum focus. For example, if it is intended to teach about enzyme kinetics, *Enzyme Kinetics*, (Heydeman and McCormick, 1982), a simulation which allows students to explore the effects of initial enzyme and substrate volumes, pH values, and temperature on enzyme activity, probably has an appropriate curriculum focus. In a similar fashion the style of interaction that a package allows gives an indication of curriculum processes that can be supported by using the software. For example, simulations will typically support exploratory and revelatory learning, and modelling packages will support the process skills associated with the interpretation and construction of models.

Educational Software and Implicit Curriculum Issues

An implicit curriculum issue which is surprisingly common relates to the national origin of the software, as designers inevitably make design assumptions based on their own national cultures. In an evaluation of the use of CD-ROMs in schools, the British National Council for Educational Technology (NCET) identifys this as a significant issue:

The American bias in most of the available discs received widespread critical comment in both the language differences and the bias in content. In view of the pressure for higher standards of grammar and spelling, it is hard to justify the direct promotion to schools of CD-ROMs which are American in their language and spelling. (NCET, 1992 p. 15)

Many programs have a cultural bias of this nature. In some cases the bias is evident — simulations of climatic systems written by Australian designers will assume that January is the height of summer in contrast to European and North American expectations (see for example Cosgrove, 1986). Other cases are less obvious. *Eureka* (ITMA collaboration, 1982), a program intended to promote discussion about graph plotting, presents an illustration of a person in a bath. The person can turn the tap on and off, and insert and remove the plug. A graph of the water level in the bath is plotted against time and displayed on the screen. The program has been found to be very effective in sponsoring discussion about the interpretation of graphs, often generating a light hearted but very constructive classroom atmosphere. On one occasion the program was demonstrated to a group of Finnish teachers, and rather surprisingly the usual amused reaction was not forthcoming. Careful questioning by the demonstrator revealed the reason — saunas are the norm in Finland, not baths!

Apart from questions of nationalistic bias, implicit curriculum content can raise important equity issues relating to race, class and gender. Griffen, in a review of *Newsnet* (Preston and Squires, 1989), a multi-user network based package which is designed to encourage children to participate in the production of the front page of a daily newspaper, criticizes the software in this respect. While applauding the basic idea of locating 'reporters' in different national newspaper offices, as represented by different network stations, she comments:

> Setting the stories in different countries could have provided a good opportunity for a real multi-cultural dimension, but instead the most predictable stereotypes are introduced, like Carnival in the West Indies, the Loch Ness Monster in Scotland, and water shortages in Africa — what a waste. (Griffen, 1989 p. 45)

Educational Software and Absent Curriculum Issues

Much software that is used in education is not designed with educational use in mind. Notably, this is the case for industry standard software, including word processors, spreadsheets, information handling packages, and desk-top publishing packages, where by default there are no curriculum aims, either implicit or explicit.

Using software which is not designed with the curriculum in mind requires the teacher to identify an appropriate curriculum focus and consider how the software could be used in the classroom. This may not be a simple task, with the need to consider subtle issues. Industry standard information handling packages typically provide very sophisticated search techniques and elaborate report formats. However, the use of such systems is complicated, requiring extensive query formulation and presentation format specification, all of which implies a detailed and lengthy interrogation process. Typically, students will test hypotheses by formulating queries quickly, expecting rapid, simply expressed results; needs which will compromise the usefulness of industry standard software.

Concerns about the educational suitability of industry standard packages have given rise to educational software packages which either express the approaches of industry standard software in an educational fashion, such as *Newspaper* (Software Production Associates, undated), a desk-top publishing package designed for use in schools, or which present industry standard software as a student edition, for example the student edition of *Lotus 1–2–3*.

Curriculum Issues in Software Assessment

Assessing software which has explicitly stated curriculum aims should be relatively straightforward, often simply requiring a comparison of these aims with a syllabus. Implicit curriculum assumptions which the designer may have made provide the selector with quite subtle assessment challenges. Assessing software which initially has no curriculum aims requires the selector to imagine how the software might be used in an educational context. In this case it is not a question of mapping the teacher's intentions onto the designer's; rather it is a matter of assessing how teachers can impose their perceptions on the software. There is a need for an assessment heuristic which will help selectors to:

(i)   identify implicit curriculum aims;

(ii) match explicit and implicit curriculum aims to perceived specific curriculum requirements;

(iii) realize the possibilities of 'subverting' explicit and implicit curriculum aims to specific curriculum requirements;

(iv) realize the educational possibilities of the use of software which initially has no explicit or implicit curriculum aims.

A useful heuristic can be developed by considering the emphasis placed on *process* or *content,* and whether the software is intended to be used in a *subject-specific* context or in a *cross-curriculum* fashion. A cross-curriculum emphasis is of particular relevance to the assessment of software for primary schools where a cross-curriculum approach is often taken. However, in secondary schools, even where the predominant emphasis is subject focused, the cross-curriculum emphasis is also important when general problem-solving skills are taught in the context of specific subjects.

Cross-Curriculum Assessment Issues

From a cross-curriculum perspective, selection should involve an assessment of how broadly based the content of the package is, and how the package can be used to support the development of general process skills.

A package with broadly based content may simply mean that the software can be used in more than one subject area. For example, *Motorway Route* (Squires and Watson, 1983), primarily designed for use in environmental studies, has been used in a number of subjects:

> *Route* took an issue which was of general interest and provided a framework within which the ideas and facts from several subject areas could be used. The program has obvious links with geography, but there are also links with other disciplines. Consideration of some of the environmental factors included a considerable amount of science. The scientific perspective was particularly evident when factors such as noise and atmospheric pollution were considered. The use of coordinates in specifying motorway routes reinforced skills; discussions helped students develop their oral language. (Squires, 1985 p. 72)

Some packages are more comprehensive in their potential application; a CD-ROM based encyclopedia can be used in more or less any area of the curriculum.

It is possible to give teachers some control over the curriculum focus of the content of a package by allowing them to incorporate content of their own choice; for example, their own data files in an information handling system, their own models in a modelling system, or their own text in a word processing system. However, not all software provides this facility. A CD-ROM encyclopedia is not designed to allow users to input their own information, it presents only fixed information. In 'fixed' software, it is important to be aware of the extent to which it is comprehensive.

The assessment of specific content may not be very important in a cross-curriculum context, as illustrated by the use of simple drills. A drill might present students with a map showing the position of a state capital, and a request to enter its name. If the name is correct another location is indicated; if the entry is incorrect, they are given another chance, and a second incorrect response results in the program supplying the correct name. The content of this program is obviously explicit, and process skills are restricted to simple memorization tasks. On the surface this is a program with very limited possibilities. However, experience has shown that such programs can act as stimuli for work with more conventional resources. In this case students have asked to use an atlas to find out more about the location of capital cities, and the software has provided a stimulus for further work with an atlas. In a similar fashion, a simple spelling drill has encouraged the use of dictionaries. In both cases software limited in content and process has encouraged students to use other resources in a more open-ended fashion, possibly promoting the acquisition of more general process skills.

The designers of *Factory* referred to in Chapter 9, epitomize attempts to use software to support general process skill development, as indicated in the documentation accompanying the package:

> If the curriculum is to change to a problem solving approach to learning, teachers must be given tools to teach problem solving techniques. The *Factory* and other Sunburst programs identify unique problem solving skills. and then put students in an environment where those skills can be utilized. (Kosel and Fish, 1983 p. 1)

It is clear that these designers are placing an emphasis on process focused work in a cross-curricular context, the subject matter in many cases simply providing a 'host' for this work.

While the subject content of *Factory* may be relatively unimportant, *The Geometric Supposer* provides an example of software designed to support the development of process skills in which the content is directly related to the curriculum. In this context, a classroom teacher who has used *The Geometric Supposer* reports:

Using *The Geometric Supposer* as part of a geometry class transforms learning geometry into making geometry. With this transformation, the balance shifts from proof to conjecture, from solutions to questions, from seeking answers to encouraging enquiry and investigation. (Schwartz *et al.*, 1985 p. 84)

An emphasis on a process focus is evident in software in which the curriculum content is absent, either as a deliberate policy as in *Logo*, or by default as in the educational use of industry standard software such as a word processor.

The claims made for *Logo* are very similar to those made for the use of *Factory*; through programming learners will be able to develop problem solving skills which will be transferable to a wide range of contexts (Papert, 1980b). However, this notion of programming skills being transferable has its critics (see for example Pea, 1987, for a discussion of the transfer of planning skills through the use of *Logo*). In this sense transfer of skills becomes an assessment issue. Based on experience of classroom use of software, selectors will need to assess how likely they feel skills transfer will be in the curriculum context they have in mind.

In an industry standard word processor there will be a full range of facilities — basic editing features such as cut and paste options, a full range of format configuration options, an extensive range of fonts, document display features, and utilities such as 'find and replace', word count and spelling check options. Assessment becomes a consideration of whether the writing processes supported by the software are those regarded as important in the students' development of writing. In this context features which support the editing of text are probably more important than presentation features. Although there is some evidence that the ability to present text in a typed format is motivating for students, it is the ability to change and edit text which has the most scope for improving writing skills. Thus an assessment of an industry standard word processor as an educational application would tend to focus on the ease with which text can be manipulated, rather than on the scope for diverse and elaborate forms of presentation.

Subject Focused Software Assessment Issues

From a subject focused perspective, selection should involve an assessment of how relevant the content of the package is to work in a specific subject, and how the package can be used to support the development of the process skills which feature in the subject area.

Assessment of content relevance for a specific subject area can be straightforward. This is illustrated by the comments made by the authors of *Human Population Growth* (Cooper and Riley, 1986), a package in a series of geography computer assisted learning units developed by the Computers in the Curriculum Project. The package relates to an established area of the curriculum. In the words of the authors: 'The study of human population growth is an important part of the curriculum for say 14 to 19 year olds and this unit provides a flexible resource to complement existing materials and courses' (Cooper and Riley, 1986 p. 7).

In terms of explicit content the selection is straightforward. Is human population growth 'on' the syllabus? Is the time required to use the program properly warranted? An obvious concern relates to how comprehensive the range of countries is. Is the selection of countries available for study sufficiently comprehensive to represent a full range of population types? The authors are obviously aware of this aspect when they state that: 'It is anticipated that teachers will want to select and modify the exercises to suit their own students' needs and interests' (Cooper and Riley, 1986 p. 7).

The need to change the explicit content to match a variety of curriculum needs is recognized through the inclusion of a section of the program which allows data corresponding to other countries to be used, and the importance with which the designers view this feature is evident in the detail with which they provide instructions on how to obtain appropriate data, and store it.

An assessment of the way in which a package can be used to support the development of process skills in a subject area can be illustrated by the design of *Human Population Growth*. As in all simulations, this program has the potential to support discovery learning, including the formulation and testing of hypotheses; obviously this is an important aspect of thinking about the implications of population growth trends. In this program the user follows a prescribed routine for the input of values; this has the benefit of supporting a systematic approach to investigation. However, it could be argued that this routine does not encourage the cross-curriculum transfer of skills such as pattern recognition and hypothesis testing to the same extent as software which allows more flexible user entry techniques (for example, through the use of a set of commands which can be invoked in any order).

Model Builder (Webb, 1991) provides further illustration of assessment issues concerned with process in a subject focused context. This package allows students to compose, run and edit computer-based models. The models are specified in an 'object oriented' fashion with models being defined in terms of three different types of 'block' — a text block, allowing elements of the model to be expressed in a purpose designed modelling language and variables to be specified; a graph block enabling results to be shown as graphs; and a picture block enabling illustrations to be presented on the screen. Models are represented on the screen as a collection of blocks, with the type of each block and any associated values displayed. When a model is run, results are computed iteratively, enabling the dynamic modelling of systems.

There is obviously no specific content in this package, and students are free to develop models in any area that they are interested in. In this sense the package is explicitly cross-curricular in nature. It is also cross-curricular in the sense that modelling is a general skill, applicable in a wide range of curriculum areas. However, the style of modelling supported by *Model Builder* is limited to dynamic modelling based on iterative solutions to mathematical equations. This is a very appropriate technique to apply to a wide range of phenomena and systems, particularly in the physical sciences, but it is not a universally appropriate technique. It is clear that an assessment of the extent to which the inherent approach to modelling is appropriate to the curriculum area in question is of critical importance.

As with curriculum content, it is possible to give teachers some control over the curriculum processes that software can be used to support, and some software incorporates mechanisms for the teacher to customize it to represent specific processes. Packages developed by the Investigations into Teaching with Microcomputers as an Aid Project epitomize this approach. The designs of these packages are based on drivecharts, a detailed and carefully worked out structure in which teachers can specify the way in which the program operates (Burkhardt, Fraser, Clowes, Eggleston, and Wells, 1982). In a similar fashion programs developed by the Computers in the Curriculum Project, which are operated by specifying keywords or commands, can be customized through the specification by the teacher of 'macro-keywords'.

Summary

In this chapter we have identified the curriculum process and content aspects of educational software as being the essential issues in considering the interaction between the perspectives of the designer and the teacher. Curriculum assumptions can be explicitly stated, or they can be implicit in the design of the software. In either case, assessment in this context is concerned with identifying and judging the appropriateness to a given educational setting of the curriculum assumptions in the software design. In some software used in education — notably software designed for use in business or industry — curriculum assumptions are absent in the design, and an important aspect of selection in these cases is to identify the potential of the package for use in educational settings. To assist in this part of the assessment task we have suggested a curriculum assessment heuristic which relates curriculum focus to the relative emphasis on process and content. This heuristic is intended to help in the formulation of specific selection questions relevant to the proposed use of the educational software package.

11 Choosing and Using Educational Software

This chapter reviews the development of the perspectives interactions paradigm and its use in software selection. The breadth of scope of the paradigm is discussed, and its application is illustrated with reference to a recently published package. We consider the robustness of the paradigm relative to developments in educational software design. In conclusion we discuss briefly an expanded use of the paradigm, particularly considering its use in educational software evaluation and educational software development.

Overview of the Perspectives Interactions Paradigm

After a review and investigation of the traditional checklist approach to selection of educational software, we rejected this as seriously limited by its focus on the attributes of software packages at the expense of consideration of educational questions. A study of the literature on software assessment revealed many reports of dissatisfaction with the checklist use for software selection, and some questioning of the use of this approach, though we could find no suggested alternative approach.

We examined some of the theoretical frameworks for studying and discussing educational software, from which checklists arose. To date these have been classificatory in nature, grouping software by application type, or educational role or rationale. We noted some limitations of these classificatory frameworks.

Then we proposed a new paradigm for thinking about educational software, based on a consideration of the interactions between pairs of the perspectives of the major actors in the use of educational software:

the student, the teacher, and the software designer. The focus on pairs of the actors jointly is distinctive in the paradigm, and powerful in its effect. It leads to an approach to software selection closely associated with software use, and emphasizing educational considerations such as classroom interactions, theories of learning processes, and curriculum issues.

In software selection, we suggest that thinking about the teacher and student perspectives interaction generates a key question of this nature: What kinds of classroom interactions and activities might be sponsored by this package? This leads to consideration of relevant issues such as classroom activities at and away from the computer, classroom climate associated with software use, student group work and possible stimulus of student-student discussion, classroom roles for teachers when software packages are used, and the possibilities for students to take greater responsibility for their own learning.

Considering the designer and student perspectives interaction raises questions about learning processes, and assumptions about these which are designed into a package, either explicitly or implicitly (or in some cases not at all). The issue of amount of control students have in the computer-based learning environment provides a way of examining this, assisted by consideration of the complexity and challenge provided by the software package.

The designer and teacher perspectives interaction raises curriculum-related issues, notably concerns with the curriculum process and content designed into a software package. These might be explicitly stated, implicit in the software, or absent in the case of software not designed originally for educational purposes. The extent to which a package might be modified to suit particular curiculum needs can also be of interest here.

We think the perspectives interactions approach enables a more comprehensive view of software selection than was indicated by the classificatory frameworks and the associated checklists. It leads away from extensive consideration of technical issues, and provides an emphasis on matters related to classroom teaching and learning. It avoids simplistic once-only ratings of software packages as 'good' or 'poor'; the value of a package can only have meaning in the context of the classroom situation in which it is to be used.

Application of the Paradigm

In this section we consider the application of the paradigm to identify selection issues relevant to the use of an example package, *The*

Multimedia Encyclopedia of Mammalian Biology (McGraw Hill, 1993). This is an interactive CD-ROM version of an existing encyclopedia of mammals. Miller (1993), in a review of the package, indicates the extent to which the designers have realized the potential of this medium. He describes the principal assets of the package as:

- The full text, colour photographs, artwork and maps of all five volumes of Grzimek's Encyclopedia of mammals, published by McGraw Hill in 1990, broken down into some 5,000 records. There are over 3,500 full-colour images and nearly 500 maps.
- Additional specialist articles to supplement the main text.
- A full glossary of terms, accessible through hypertext, comprising sections from McGraw Hill's *Dictionary of Scientific and Technical Terms.*
- Movie and sound, largely taken from the BBC Natural History Unit archives; in total there is nearly one hour of sound clips and twenty minutes of movie sequences.
- Full current bibliography of scientific literature on mammalogy.
- Dedicated navigation and retrieval software.

(Miller, 1993 p. 21)

Users can use the encyclopedia in four different modes: search, trail, compare, and browse. The search mode enables the user to interrogate the full database; the trail mode presents previously accessed records; the compare mode allows two simultaneous views of two different records; and the browse mode a choice of four different 'browsers' — Table of Contents (as in the original paper version of the encyclopedia), Taxonomic, Biogeographic, and Thematic.

Thinking about the Teacher-Student Interaction

This interaction is concerned with the kinds of classroom activities that might be sponsored by a package. Miller describes the encyclopedia as 'resourceware', and this description is indicative of some of the ways in which this package can be used with students. In Chapter 8 we stated that a significant concern in the context of this interaction can be the extent to which students take responsibility for their own learning. Software which provides students with a resource of this kind can be used effectively to encourage students to take on more of this responsibility; by giving them access to a source of information other than the teacher they can become more autonomous.

The comprehensive nature of the encyclopedia has some effect on the teacher's role. There will be more emphasis on the teacher as manager and facilitator of the learning activities, as students need to learn to use a resource such as this effectively. We are all familiar with the superficial nature of students' projects consisting of sections copied from an encyclopedia or reference book. Students' research questions, searching skills, analysis of information obtained from the encyclopedia, and reporting of their discoveries, will all need to be guided and given some structure in classroom activities devised by the teacher.

Thinking about the Designer-Student Interaction

Thinking about learner control, complexity and challenge should enable a selector to form an opinion of the theory of learning underpinning this package. The diverse forms of interrogation that the student can use indicate that the package has been designed to give students significant control over their use of the package. A package with 5,000 records, 3,500 full-colour images, nearly 500 maps, specialist articles, a full glossary of terms, movie and sound, and a full current bibliography of scientific literature on mammalogy, would seem to be inherently complex, providing diverse possibilities for interacting with the software. The use of the package can support quite involved and complicated problem-solving activities, providing challenging experiences for the students. In summary, the package seems to allow significant learner control within a complex and challenging environment; a description that indicates a constructivist view of learning.

This assessment is confirmed by the editors of the package. In his review of the package Miller quotes them as claiming:

> The user becomes an active participant in the learning process, firmly in change of the learning experience. Moreover, through seeing, hearing and doing, the user finds that learning not only becomes more absorbing and enjoyable — the ability to remember information and make conceptual links is also dramatically increased.
>
> (Miller, 1993 p. 21)

It is evident from this that the designers view learning from a constructivist point of view; learner control is emphasized and students having the opportunity to make conceptual links is seen as an element of learning.

Thinking about the Designer-Teacher Interaction

The ways in which the encyclopedia can be browsed indicate that the designers have deliberately tried to cater for the needs of subject specialists. The four browsers which are available are: Table of Contents (as in the original paper version of the encyclopedia), Taxonomic, Biogeographic, and Thematic. The first browser is obviously a reflection of the origins of the package, while the remaining three are geared specifically to the search processes that biologists might typically employ. In this sense the package is designed to support curriculum specific processes. However, there is also the possibility that its use may support more broadly based skills; a possibility which is implicit in the identification by the editors of three anticipated ways of using the package — looking-up, exploring, and testing hypotheses. There is a possibility that expertise gained in exercising any one of these in the restricted context of mammalian biology might be transferable to other curriculum contexts.

The content of the package evidently aims to be comprehensive within a specific area of study. A proper assessment of how comprehensive the content is would obviously require a detailed in-depth examination of the package, but the number of records, illustrations and maps suggest that this is indeed a comprehensive piece of work. In addition the package appears to be comprehensive in another respect; a wide range of presentation formats (text, video, slides, audio) are used, which is very appropriate to the multi-faceted nature of the subject matter. It is possible to prioritize the screen display in terms of text, image, sound or video.

Quite clearly this package is specific to a well-defined area of the curriculum and should be assessed with this in mind. As with all CD-ROM products the information is fixed, and the scope of such packages is correspondingly limited. A combination of this subject focus and the fixed nature of the CD-ROM format, leads to some paradoxical concerns. On the one hand, the CD-ROM based encyclopedia appears to be comprehensive both in terms of content and process, providing access to a large amount of information in diverse formats and capable of supporting a range of processes associated with the searching of information. On the other hand, it is not possible to enter new information or edit existing material, the material is focused very clearly on a limited aspect of the curriculum, and the search processes are geared to the typical needs of biologists. In the case of this package a primary concern in selection is whether tightly defined information and specifically tuned search processes are what are required to support perceived curriculum aims.

The Paradigm and Future Developments

In discussing the perspectives interactions paradigm we have referred both to educational software that was developed some time ago and to software that has only recently been produced. This has been a deliberate policy, intended to demonstrate that the paradigm will not date as the sophistication of the design and use of educational software increases. The references to the use of packages and to related classroom issues that we have made throughout the book have demonstrated the validity of the paradigm in 'new' and 'old' software contexts. This is in sharp contrast to the use of other assessment techniques, which need to be 'tinkered' with to address new developments. The classic example of this is provided by the design of specific checklists to be used for different types of software; as the design rationales for educational software increase the number of checklists will increase correspondingly. On the other hand, if a general checklist is used, the list will get longer and longer or need to be altered in other ways in an effort to accommodate new developments.

The capacity of the paradigm to cope with future, as yet unspecified, developments is one of its major strengths. This capacity is due to its generative nature. The perspectives interactions paradigm does not list specific questions; rather it provides a mechanism for generating context specific issues and questions when, and as, they are required. These issues and questions are based on fundamental educational roles involved in the use of educational software, and are thus not predicated on largely irrelevant technical concerns. In this way, the paradigm will be able to generate appropriate issues and questions when applied to future software, as the fundamental educational aims do change, and the specific issues and questions will be generated within the context of the use of the software in classrooms of the future.

Scope of the Paradigm

We have developed the perspectives interactions paradigm primarily to provide a principled approach to software selection, and we have discussed at length the significance of this paradigm both in providing a fully developed way of thinking about software selection, and as a

Interaction between perspectives	Assessment issues	
	Selection	Evaluation
Teacher/student	(i) Implied role(s) of the teacher in the classroom. (ii) Expectations of the nature of classroom interactions (iii) Customization: pedagogy	(i) Actual role(s) of the teacher in the classroom (ii) Observed nature of classroom interactions (iii) Customization: pedagogy
Designer/student	(i) Implicit/explicit/absent theories of learning (ii) User (student) access features	(i) Appropriateness and effectiveness of theories of learning (ii) Ease and extent of user (student) access.
Designer/teacher	(i) Implicit/explicit/absent curriculum aims: content and process (ii) Customization: content.	(i) Customization: content.

Figure 11.1   The perspectives interactions paradigm applied to software evaluation

mechanism for generating assessment heuristics. However, we think that the use of this paradigm is not limited to software selection. It provides some basis for software evaluation, and it can be applied even more broadly to provide a general way of thinking about the use of educational software in schools.

First, we will consider the use of the paradigm to assist in software evaluation. In Chapter 1 we made a clear distinction between selection and evaluation. Selection was defined as the assessment of software by teachers in anticipation of its use with groups of students in classrooms or with individual students, while evaluation was defined as assessment of software based on the actual observation of the use of the software. This distinction can be related to the perspectives paradigm as shown in Figure 11.1.

Looking first at the teacher-student interaction and selection it can be seen that there is a need to assess the software in terms of implied roles for the teacher and expectations of the nature of classroom inter-actions sponsored by the software. Of course it is very difficult to make these assessments, based as they are on surmise and anticipation. In considering this interaction in an evaluation context, the crucial differ-ence is that assessment of roles and classroom interactions is now based on observations of actual practice rather that anticipated outcomes. The ability to customize software to reflect different teaching styles is of importance, as this will allow teachers to adapt software to anticipated classroom needs identified during selection, and to reflect the results of evaluation. Selection and the designer-student-interaction involves two major assessment strands: identifying theories of learning which are either implicit or explicit in the software design, and judging the suitability of user interface features. Evaluation in the context of this interaction is concerned with an assessment of the observed effectiveness of the implicit or explicit theories of learning as made available by the software, and the ease with which students can actually use the software. Considering the designer-teacher interaction for selection leads to an assessment of implicit and explicit curriculum relevance, both in terms of the content and process. The ability to customize software to reflect varying content is important for incorporating material that is identified as being appropriate during selection, and in adapting content on the basis of evaluation.

Considering broader issues, we turn our attention to the design and development of educational software. One of the most difficult aspects of educational software design is the development of a perception of significant and realistic use of software in the classroom. In a sense, design is an inverse of selection; a selector often has to make an informed guess of the designer's intentions and map them on to anticipated classroom use, while the designer has to guess at likely realizable classroom uses and develop a design accordingly. We think that in considering the three perspectives interactions a designer will be able to develop a more insightful and comprehensive approach to design, incorporating better understanding of classroom uses of educational software.

Thinking about the two perspectives interactions involving the designer (the designer-student and the designer-teacher interactions) will help the designer to focus on essential aspects of good software design — the proper use of theories of learning as a basis for design, and an awareness of curriculum issues. While the designer may well be aware of these considerations, the act of deliberately focusing on questions raised within the context of these interactions will assist articulation of a principled and thorough approach to design.

While the two designer related interactions can provide significant assistance to the designer, the help there is essentially clarifying and expressing ideas and concepts with which the designer will be familiar. The assistance rendered by considering the teacher-student interaction is different in character, bringing a novel contribution to the design and development process. The questions and issues raised in the context of this interaction are about the social and off-computer interactions between teachers and students. This is an aspect of design which is often not given enough attention, and using the paradigm will help designers to pay proper regard to these issues.

In an even broader context, we feel that the paradigm has much to offer in developing a general critical awareness of the issues and concepts associated with using educational software. By this we mean that the paradigm can be used to assist thinking and discussion in this area. All too often, discussion about the use of computers in schools is couched in extravagant and enthusiastic terms, and fails to address fundamental issues. Similarly, much of the discussion is technocentric, focusing on the latest hardware developments, with scant regard for educational concerns. The perspectives interactions paradigm can provide an antidote to extravagant technocentric approaches, offering a sound theoretical basis for discussion which focuses on educational aspects of software use.

Appendixes

Appendix A
Courseware Evaluation Form (MicroSIFT, 1982)

MICROSIFT EVALUATORS GUIDE JANUARY 1982

Northwest
Regional
Educational
Laboratory

micro**SIFT**

COURSEWARE DESCRIPTION

PACKAGE TITLE _____

VERSION _____ COST _____

PRODUCER/DATE _____

SUBJECT AREA _____ GRADE/ABILITY LEVEL _____

SPECIFIC TOPIC _____

DEWEY DECIMAL/LIBRARY OF CONGRESS # _____

SEARS SUBJECT HEADING(S) _____

ERIC DESCRIPTORS _____

MEDIUM OF TRANSFER: ☐ Tape Cassette ☐ 5" Flex. Disk
                    ☐ ROM Cartridge ☐ 8" Flex. Disk

REQUIRED HARDWARE:

REQUIRED SOFTWARE:

TYPE OF PACKAGE: ☐ Single Program ☐ Integrated program
                                      series component

INSTRUCTIONAL PURPOSE: (Please check all applicable)
☐ Remediation ☐ Standard Instruction ☐ Enrichment

INSTRUCTIONAL TECHNIQUES: (Please check all applicable descriptions)
☐ Drill and Practice ☐ Game ☐ Learning Management
☐ Tutorial ☐ Simlation ☐ Utility
☐ Information Retrieval ☐ Problem Solving ☐ Other

DOCUMENTATION AVAILABLE: Circle *all* that are available in the computer program (P) or in the supplementary materials (S).

S S Suggested grade/ability level(s)   P S Teacher's information

P S Instructional objectives   P S Resource/reference info.

P S Prerequisite skills or activities   P S Student's instructions

P S Sample program output   P S Student worksheets

P S Program operating instructions   P S Relationship to standard textbooks

P S Pre-test   P S Follow-up activities

P S Post-test   P S Other _____

IS LISTING AND ALTERATION OF THE COMPUTER PROGRAM

PRODUCER'S FIELD-TEST DATA IS AVAILABLE

☐ ON REQUEST

☐ WITH THE PACKAGE

☐ NOT AVAILABLE

ESTIMATE THE EXPECTED TIME OF STUDENT INTERACTION WITH THE PACKAGE NEEDED TO ACHIEVE THE OBJECTIVES. (CAN BE STATED AS TOTAL TIME, TIME PER DAY, TIME RANGE OR OTHER INDICATOR.)

INSTRUCTIONAL OBJECTIVES: ☐ Stated   ☐ Inferred

INSTRUCTIONAL PREREQUISITES: ☐ Stated   ☐ Inferred

DESCRIBE PACKAGE CONTENT AND STRUCTURE (INCLUDING RECORD-KEEPING AND REPORTING FUNCTIONS):

RATING: Circle the letter abbreviation which best reflects your judgment.
(Use the space following each item for comments.)

IMPORTANCE: Circle the letter which reflects your judgment of the relative importance of the item in this evaluation.

☐ Check this box if the evaluation is based partly on your observation of student use of this package.

PACKAGE TITLE _____

REVIEWER'S NAME _____

VERSION _____

DATE OF REVIEW _____

COURSEWARE EVALUATION

Northwest Regional Educational Laboratory

RATING
SA — Strongly agree
A — Agree
D — Disagree
SD — Strongly disagree
NA — Not Applicable

IMPORTANCE (optional)
H — Higher
L — Lower

	RATING	IMPORTANCE	
CONTENT			
	SA A D SD NA	H L	1. The content is accurate. (p.15)
	SA A D SD NA	H L	2. The content has educational value. (p.15)
	SA A D SD NA	H L	3. The content is free of race, ethnic, sex, and other stereotypes. (p.16)
	SA A D SD NA	H L	4. The purpose of the package is well-defined. (p.16)
	SA A D SD NA	H L	5. The package achieves its defined purpose. (p.16)
	SA A D SD NA	H L	6. Presentation of content is clear and logical. (p. 33)
	SA A D SD NA	H L	7. The level of difficulty is appropriate for the target audience. (p. 33)
INSTRUCTIONAL QUALITY	SA A D SD NA	H L	8. Graphics/color/sound are used for appropriate instructional reasons. (p. 34)
	SA A D SD NA	H L	9. Use of the package is motivational. (p. 34)
	SA A D SD NA	H L	10. The package effectively stimulates student creativity. (p. 34)
	SA A D SD NA	H L	11. Feedback on student responses is effectively employed. (p. 35)
	SA A D SD NA	H L	12. The learner controls the rate and sequence of presentation and review. (p. 36)
	SA A D SD NA	H L	13. Instruction is integrated with previous student experience. (p. 36)
	SA A D SD NA	H L	14. Learning is generalizable to an appropriate range of situations. (p. 36)

TECHNICAL QUALITY	SA A D SD NA	H	L	15. The user support materials are comprehensive. (p. 37)
	SA A D SD NA	H	L	16. The user support materials are effective. (p. 38)
	SA A D SD NA	H	L	17. Information displays are effective. (p. 39)
	SA A D SD NA	H	L	18. Intended users can easily and independently operate the program. (p. 40)
	SA A D SD NA	H	L	19. Teachers can easily employ the package. (p. 41)
	SA A D SD NA	H	L	20. The program appropriately uses relevant computer capabilities. (p. 42)
	SA A D SD NA	H	L	21. The program is reliable in normal use. (p. 42)

microSIFT

22. (Check one only) (p. 43)
☐ I would use or recommend use of this package with little or no change.
    (Note suggestions for effective use under Section 25.)
☐ I would use or recommend use of this package only if certain changes were made.
    (Note recommended changes under Section 24.)
☐ I would not use or recommend this package. (Note reasons under Section 24.)

23. Describe the major strengths of the package. (p. 43)

24. Describe the major weaknesses of the package. (p. 44)

25. Describe the potential use of the package in classroom settings. (p. 44)

Appendix B
Software Evaluation Proforma (Salvas and Thomas, 1982)

SOFTWARE EVALUATION

Reviewer ....   Date............................

Name of Program..   Version.......................

Author ....

Manufacturer/Distributor ....

Cost $

Subject/Course ....

Age/Year Level ....

Brand of Machine ....   Memory Required .... K

Disc Drives Required (No.) ....   Printer   (Y / N)

Application Type ....

Teacher Notes   Poor 1 2 3 4 5 Excellent

Student Notes   Poor 1 2 3 4 5 Excellent

Are sample results provided?   (Y / N)

If so, rate them   Poor 1 2 3 4 5 Excellent

Is the documentation easily understood?   (Y / N)

TEACHER EVALUATION CRITERIA

Educational Criteria
Does the program:
(a)	fit my syllabus?	Y / N
(b)	have a clearly defined topic?	Y / N
(c)	match my educational philosophy?	Y / N
(d)	use the same methodology for all students?	Y / N
(e)	suit a variety of users?	Y / N
(f)	suit the group I have in mind?	Y / N
(g)	develop social skills?	Y / N
(h)	suit (please tick)	

        (i)   individual use   [ ]
        (ii)   small groups   [ ]
        (iii)   large group   [ ]
        (iv)   whole class   [ ]

User Reaction
Does the program:
(a)	motivate the user?	Y / N
(b)	allow student interaction?	Y / N

Screen Criteria
(a)	Is the display easily read?	Y / N
(b)	Is the language appropriate for my students?	Y / N
(c)	Is the nature of the user input clearly indicated?	Y / N

Functional Criteria
(a)	Is the program easy to start?	Y / N
(b)	Are input errors easily corrected?	Y / N
(c)	Does incorrect data entry cause termination of the program?	Y / N
(d)	Can students use the program independently?	Y / N
(e)	Does the program access the disc during the program's operation?	Y / N

Machine exploitation
(a)   Does the software make good use of the computer's features?   Y / N

Supplementary Materials
(a)   Do the worksheets provide a useful follow-up to the program?   Y / N
(b)   Does the program provide useful feedback to the teacher?   Y / N

STUDENT EVALUATION CRITERIA

Educational Criteria
(a)   Is the structure of the program flexible for the user?   Y / N
(b)   Is diagnostic assistance part of the program?   Y / N

Functional Criteria
(a)   Are the instructions clear?   Y / N
(b)   Can the user recall the instructions?   Y / N
(c)   Can the user control rate of delivery and level of difficulty?   Y / N

Machine Exploitation
(a)   Are special effects wisely used?   Y / N

Supplementary Materials
(a)   Do the worksheets provide meaningful activities?   Y / N

Your reactions to the program including further comments on any of the above questions.

....

....

....

....

....

Appendix C
Guidelines for Evaluating Software in Reading (Krause, condensed and cited in Miller and Burnett, 1986)

(1)   Will the company send the material on approval?

(2)   Is there a warranty on the software?

(3)   Are color graphics and sound used effectively?

(4)   Can students be assigned a specific skill from the program?

(5)   Does the software use a game format?

(6)   Are the directions written clearly?

(7)   Is there a record keeping or record management system?

(8)   Can a printout of the student's performance be made?

(9)   Is the vocabulary and density of concepts appropriate for the level?

(10) Does the program allow for flexible reading rates?

(11) Is the program free from race, ethnic or other stereotypes?

(12) If the vendor makes improvements, can updated versions be acquired cheaply or free?

Appendix D
Guidelines for Educational Software Evaluation
(Coburn, 1985)

Program Content

Is the content of the materials suitable for your students?
Does the content of the materials fit with your curricular goals?
What values does the content convey?
Is the content contained in the materials accurate?
Is the content educationally significant?
Are the goals and objectives of the materials explicitly or implicitly
    clear?

Pedagogy

What is the nature of the feedback the program provides to students?
What assumptions about learning and how children learn are built into
    the software?
Does the software permit modification to meet individual student needs?
Is the software package self-contained, or does it require teacher inter-
    vention?
Can the program be used with various types of class arrangements
    (individual, small group, whole class)?
Does the program tap a variety of learning modes (visual, aural, nu-
    merical, verbal)?

Program Operation

Is the program free of bugs and breaks?
How does the program handle user errors?
How much control does the user have over the program operation?
Are directions in the program itself clear and acceptable?
Is there good clear documentation for the teacher?
Is there good clear documentation for students?
How well does the program use graphics, sound, and color capabilit-
    ies?
Are screen displays effective?

Student Outcomes

How easy is the program for students to use?
Is the program interesting to students?

Does the program make appropriate use of limited computer resources?
Do students enjoy using the programs?
How well do students learn what the program is intended to teach?
What, if any, unintended learning results from using the program?
How effective is this program compared with non-computer instruction
in the same area?

Appendix E
Software Selection Criteria (Preece and Jones, 1985)

1 Educational Documentation

a Statement of aims and objectives
b Information about the content and background
c Statement of intended type of use and audience
d Suggestion of ways to use the program
e Pupils activities or worksheets
f Instructions for running the program
g Presentation of a typical run
h General impressions

2 Achievement of Stated Aims
(as far as you can tell without actually using the program)

a Aims/objectives
b General impressions

3 Appropriateness of the Micro and Program

a For teaching this topic
b For the suggested audience and type of use
c General impressions

4 Screen Presentation

a Use of graphics
b Use of colour and animation
c General impressions

5 Friendliness and Flexibility of the Program

a Helpful messages to correct user errors
b Help to pupils in understanding the program

    c   Versatility so that the user can control what the program does
    d   Feedback to pupils
    e   Program adapts to pupils' performance
    f   Record of pupils' performance kept by program
    g   Program model accessible to pupil
    h   Suggestions or help for teacher to modify the program
    i   General impressions

6 Technical Documentation

    a   Information about machine requirements
    b   Information about the model used
    c   Information about the program structure
    d   Listing and readability of the program code
    e   Portability, i.e. ability to transfer program to a different computer
    f   General impressions

Appendix F
An edited version of the Checklist from the article
'Evaluating Software for the Classroom' (Reay, 1985)

A two-stage approach should be used. The first stage should be carried out by the teacher(s) working through the program documentation and the program itself. The second should involve the teacher(s) watching one or at most two children of appropriate age or stage of learning, using the program under classroom conditions.

Stage 1

Section A: Management

1   Is the program available on disc, tape, EPROM or all three?
2   Are any ancillary pieces of hardware necessary (e.g. a printer)?
3   Is a user's guide provided?
4   If provided, is the user's guide
        (a)   easy to read?
        (b)   easy to access information?
5   Does the user's guide include the following information?
        (a)   an overview of the program, including a statement of what kind of program it claims to be, e.g. drill and practice, concept teaching, and so on.

(b) a statement of the learning objective.

(c) a description of program operation and how to handle problems which may arise.

(d) a statement of any prerequisite skills or knowledge.

(e) a 'diagnostic' pre-measure.

(f) some form of checking whether the user learns anything as a result of using the program.

(g) details of any other materials required.

(h) any difficulties which may occur when making a work copy of the original program?

6 Are the operating procedures consistent throughout?

7 Is sufficient information to operate the program provided on screen?

8 If not, is written material provided which provides the guidance necessary?

9 To what extent is the program under user control?

Section B: Educational Aspects of the Program

11 What kind of program does it claim to be?

12 What kind of program is it?

13 Is what the program claims to teach (e.g. problem-solving, calculating area, punctuation) worth teaching?

14 Does the approach fit in with your aims?

15 Does the content fit in with learning objectives for your class?

16 Can the teaching or practice which the program claims to provide be achieved more efficiently through a more traditional approach?

17 Is the program concerned with:

(a) Concept learning? See Section C below.

(b) Rule learning? See Section D below.

(c) Memory training? See Section E below.

(d) Problem-solving? See Section F below.

(e) Practice? See Section G below.

Section C: If Concept Learning

18 Most or all of the following elements should be present — are they?

(a) a definition or statement identifying the critical attributes.

(b) 'matching' exercises involving examples and non-examples.

(c) 'attribute isolation' — the use of attention-focusing devices which isolate critical attributes.

(d)   'contrast practice'.
(e)   single discriminations before mixed up.
(f)   examples tied to learners' past experience.
(g)   gradual reduction in the scale of differences between examples.
(h)   to show that the concept has been learned, are novel unencountered instances used as tests?

Section D: If Rule Learning

19   All or most of the following should be in evidence — are they?
(a)   the performance expected of the learner.
(b)   presentation of the rule.
(c)   provision of examples.
(d)   opportunities for practice.
(e)   ample and appropriate feedback.
(f)   opportunity for the learner to demonstrate acquisition of the rule.
(g)   integrated view of the rule.

Section E: If Memory Training

20   The following should be present — are they?
(a)   does the content mean anything to the intended audience?
(b)   is repetition used?
(c)   is the repetition appropriate?
(d)   is the organization of the content clear to the learner?
(e)   do related items appear close to each other in time and/ or space?
(f)   are the number of new items presented in range 3–7?
(g)   will the consequences of learning be of meaning to the learner?
(h)   are all correct responses reinforced during the early stages?
(i)   there should be no negative feedback in the early stages.

Section F: If Problem-Solving

21   The following should be present — are they?
(a)   a clear description of the pre-knowledge required — in terms of processes understood rather than procedures learned.

(b) information to the learner about what is to be achieved.

(c) instructions which encourage the learner to discover a solution him/herself.

(d) instructions which stimulate recall of relevant rules or methods of solution.

Section G: If Practice

22 Ask the following questions:

(a) has the subject matter which is to be practised already been taught?

(b) have the children reached the point of requiring practice?

(c) is the nature of the practice appropriate to the content taught?

(d) is the feedback positive?

(e) is revision teaching included in the program?

(f) is a performance record provided which gives diagnostic information?

(g) is interference introduced?

When you have completed this section you will be in a position to decide whether the programme looks promising or whether it simply does not fit the needs of your class. If the latter you should go no further. If it looks reasonable, move to Stage 2.

Stage 2

To be carried out with one or at most two children who are members of the group who will use the program if it is selected.

1 Can the child read and understand any documentation which is essential for easy use of the program?

2 Can the child start the program without assistance?

3 Is it clear to the child what he/she is expected to do throughout the program?

4 Can the child operate the program easily with the information provided?

5 Can the child access on-screen instructions from any point in the program?

6 Does the program introduce interference?

7 Does the program capture and hold attention?

8 Can the child operate the program the way he/she would prefer?

9 Is the organization of the content obvious to the child?

Appendix G
Choosing Software (Templeton, 1985)

Basic Considerations

Will it run on my machine?
Does it require any peripherals?
Does the publisher have a good name?
Does the program run?
Is it robust?
Does it contain spelling errors?
Is it easy to use?
Is it well packaged?
Is it well documented?
Is it well presented?

Educational Considerations

Was the program written by, or in conjunction with, a teacher of the
relevant subject?
Is there reference, in the documentation, to a current syllabus, or to
other educational materials?
Is the program writer, or the producer, or the publisher associated with
an established educational organization?
Does it look as though the program's approach or level would be
suitable for your child?
Is is something you would be wanting your child to do in any case? In
other words, if you wouldn't dream of making your daughter sit
down to do ten sums with pencil and paper, don't consider asking
her to do it with a computer!
Will it put the child in control of the computer, or will it attempt to put
the computer in control of the child?

Special Considerations

Does it take advantage of the capabilities of the computer?
Is it flexible?
Will it hold the child's attention?
Does it allow the child control of what is happening?

Appendix H
Educational Software Selection Criteria (Blease, 1986)

CHOOSING EDUCATIONAL SOFTWARE: GENERAL SELECTION CRI-
TERIA

Documentation

(i)   Technical
      Does the program have any accompanying documentation?
      Are there any simple loading and running instructions?
      Does the program require anything other than the most element-
         ary knowledge of the computer to get it up and running?
      Are hardware requirements made explicit in the simplest of
         terms?
      Are instructions given for making a back-up copy of the tape or
         disc? If not, do the publishers offer a replacement service for
         corrupted discs and tapes?
      Does the documentation include a list of other machines for which
         a version of the program is available?
(ii) Program information
      Are the aims and objectives of the program made clear?
      Does it specify the age and ability range for which it was de-
         signed: What degree of flexibility does it provide?
      What kind of program is it?
      Does the program allow for any alterations to be made? If so, are
         the instructions unambiguous and easy for the non-expert to
         follow?
      Does the documentation contain instructions for a 'browse mode'
         or details of a 'sample run'?

Presentation and Layout

Are instructions clear and unambiguous?
Is each frame attractively presented avoiding irrelevant detail?
Have coloured and double height characters been used to their best
      advantage?
Is the use of graphics appropriate to the aims and objectives of the
      program?

If pictures and diagrams are included, could they be represented more effectively by some other means? e.g. a printed sheet, a map or a photograph.

If sound effects are included, do they constitute an essential and integral part of the program?

Does the program provide a simple means whereby the volume can be controlled or the sound can be turned off completely?

Friendliness and Flexibility

Does the program provide helpful messages to correct errors?

Is sufficient help provided so that pupils can understand the program without your constant intervention?

Is the program sufficiently versatile so that the user can control what it does?

Is the program sufficiently flexible to be applicable in a variety of teaching/learning situations?

Achievement of Stated Aims

Without actually using the program, and keeping your own pupils in mind, to what extent do you think the program would achieve its/ your aims and objectives?

Robustness

Is it easy for the user to correct typing errors?

Are possible errors trapped? When numerical input is required, what happens if you type in a word? What happens if you type in a number when a word is required?

When textual input is required, what is the longest sentence you can input? Does the program crash if you enter a longer one?

Can you get all the way through the program without entering anything, just pressing the RETURN key each time a word, number or sentence is required?

When numerical input is required, what happens if you type in very large or very small numbers?

Can the program cope with an input of zero or a negative number?

Are all non-essential keys automatically turned off by the program itself? Try pressing some wrong keys, e.g. ESCAPE BREAK SHIFT/ BREAK, the CONTROL key in conjunction with any others.

Choosing Educational Software — Specific Selection Criteria

(i)   Tutorial and Drill and Practice Programs

Is the content fully described?

Is the content of the program appropriate to the designer's stated aims and objectives?

Is the content and presentation appropriate to your class and the use you have in mind?

Is the micro appropriate for teaching this topic?

Is the content/information accurate?

Is the content/information accurate enough for the use you have in mind?

Does the input format suit your purposes? Are there options from which you can choose?

Does the program provide immediate and appropriate feedback to the user?

Does the program keep a score or a record of the learner's progress?

Does the program suggest pencil and paper tasks, or other work that might be carried out away from the computer?

For Tutorial programs in particular

Is the content broken down into appropriately small and logical stages?

Does the program allow the user to revise previous pages or follow remedial loops?

Will the program take free-format answers in an acceptable number of forms?

For Drill and Practice programs in particular

Does the program provide a variety of levels of difficulty?

Are the examples or exercises randomly generated?

(ii)   Arcade-type games

Are the instructions clear and always available?

Does the program provide a sufficient range of levels of difficulty and speed?

Is the content of the program available for inspection and/or change?

Is the content accurate?
Does the program provide appropriate feedback to the player?
Does the program keep a score or a record of the player's progress?
Is the visual display likely to be attractive, exciting and absorbing?

(iii) Simulation games

Is it appropriate to use the computer for this topic?
Is the content of the program appropriate to your aims and to the group you have in mind?
Are commands and instructions available throughout the program run?
Does the program (or the documentation) give sufficient and appropriate clues if the user gets stuck?
Is the nature of the model made explicit?
Is there provision to change data if appropriate?
Can a game be 'saved' and resumed later?
Does the program give any suggestions as to how it might relate to events in the real world?

(iv) Laboratory simulations

Is the nature of the mathematical model made specific?
Is the range and degree of accuracy of the model discussed in the documentation?
Is there provision for changing the data?
Could this topic be covered more effectively with real practical work?

(v) Content-free tools

Data-bases

When creating files

Are the instructions clear and easy to follow?
What is the maximum number of records and fields?
What is the maximum field size?
Is there an option to edit and delete records?
Can the number of records be increased after the file has been created?

When interrogating files

Are the instructions for formulating a query clear and unambiguous?

Is there a 'help' option to explain the commands and to describe the fields?

Does the search option allow you to formulate both simple and complex queries?

What is the longest query acceptable?

Appendix I
Characteristics Considered in Evaluating Educational Software (OTA, 1988)

Characteristics Considered in Evaluating Educational Software.

Based on items used by 36 public, private, and governmental software evaluation agencies, and additional items considered important by selected teachers, software publishers, university professors, and private consultants.

Instructional Quality

General

Program is useful in a school-based, instructional setting (i.e. in a classroom, computer laboratory, media center, or school library).

Program avoids potentially controversial, nonstandard teaching methodologies.

Program allows completion of a lesson in one class period (approximately 30 minutes).

Instruction is integrated with previous student experience.

Program is likely to save time for the student when compared to other means of presenting this topic.

Program is likely to save time for the teacher when compared to other means of presenting this topic.

An on-disk tutorial concerning the program's command structure is provided when appropriate (e.g. for a word processing program).

Content

Content is appropriate for intended student population.

Content is accurate.

Content is current.

Content breadth is reasonable (does not focus on too few or too many different concepts or content topics within one session).

The processes and information learned are useful in domains other than the subject area of the program.

Content is free of grammar, spelling, punctuation, and usage errors.

Content is free of any bias or stereotyping.

Content supports the school curriculum.

Content is relevant to the subject field.

Definitions are provided when necessary.

There is continuity between the information presented and prerequisite skills required.

Content avoids taking a side on potentially controversial moral or social issues.

There is a need for better than the standard treatment of this topic in the curriculum.

Appropriateness

Application is well suited to computer use.

The pedagogic approach used is superior to what is available elsewhere.

Readability level is appropriate for the intended student population.

Tone of address is appropriate for the intended student population.

The means of response (e.g. single keystroke, manipulating graphics) is appropriate to the intended student population.

Prerequisite skills required are appropriate for the intended student population.

Time required for use by a typical student does not exceed the attention span of that student.

Multiple levels of instruction are available.

Difficulty levels are based on discernible logic (e.g. reading ability, complexity of problems).

Sufficient exposure and practice are provided to master skills.

Sufficient information is presented for intended learning to occur.

Questioning Techniques

Questions are appropriate to the content and effectively measure student mastery of the content.

Questions incorrectly answered can be repeated later in the lesson/exercise.

The number of trials are reasonable and appropriate (e.g. student receives the correct answer after no more than three or four trials, and after at least two trials).

Calculation can be accomplished easily on-screen when appropriate.

Approach/Motivation

Approach is appropriate for the intended student population.
Format is varied.
Overall tenor of interaction is helpful.
Student is an active participant in the learning process.

Evaluator's Field Test Results

Student understands the on-screen presentation, and can proceed without confusion or frustration.
Student enjoys using the program.
Student retains a positive attitude about using the program.
Student retains the desire to use the program again, or to pursue the topic in other ways.
Program involves students in competition in a positive way.
Program fosters cooperation among students.

Creativity

Program challenges and stimulates creativity.
Pedagogy is innovative.
Program allows the student as many decisions as possible.
Program provides opportunities to answer open-ended questions and provides evaluative criteria to assess responses.
Program demonstrates a creative way of using knowledge.
Program challenges the student to alter an underlying model, or design an alternative model.

Learner Control

Learner can alter program sequence and pace.
Learner can review instructions and previous frames.
Learner can end activity any time and return to main menu.
Learner can enter program at different points.
Learner can stop in the midst of an activity, and at a later session begin at that stopping point with the previous record of progress intact.
Help is available at likely points of need.

Learning Objectives, Goals and Outcomes

Learner objectives are stated and purpose is well defined.
Steps are taken to make learning generalizable to other situations.
For programs requiring use over several days, learning outcomes are worth the time invested.

Feedback

Feedback is positive.

Feedback is appropriate to the intended student population and does not threaten or inadvertently reward incorrect responses.

Feedback is relevant to student responses.

Feedback is timely.

Feedback is informative.

Feedback is corrective when appropriate.

Feedback remediates and/or explains when appropriate.

Feedback employs a variety of responses to student input, and avoids being boring or unnecessarily detailed.

Feedback remains on the screen for an appropriate amount of time.

Branching is used effectively to remediate.

Program uses branching to automatically adjust difficulty levels or sequence according to student performance.

Simulations

Simulation model is valid and neither too complex nor too simple for intended student population.

Variables used in the simulation are the most relevant.

Variables in the simulation interact and produce results approximately as they would in real life.

Assumptions are adequately identified.

Program simulates activities that can be too difficult, dangerous, or expensive to demonstrate in reality.

The time needed to complete both a step and the entire simulation is reasonable and effective.

Encourages decision making or calculation rather than guessing.

Teacher Modifiability

Teacher can easily change or add content.

Teacher can easily regulate parameters (e.g. number of problems, rate of presentation, percentage correct needed for mastery) for each class using the program.

Teacher can easily regulate parameters (e.g. number of problems, rate of presentation, percentage correct needed for mastery) for each student.

Parameter set-ups can be by-passed (e.g. default settings are available).

Evaluation and Recordkeeping

Program provides an adequate means of evaluating student mastery of the content.

If tests are included, criteria for success are appropriate for the ability/ skills of the intended student population.

If tests are included, content accurately reflects the material presented.

Scorekeeping and performance reports are provided for the student when appropriate (e.g. summary of problems correct/number attempted, running point totals).

Useful information about student performance is stored for future retrieval.

Useful diagnostic pre-test or placement test is provided, where appropriate.

Useful diagnostic or prescriptive analysis of student performance is available to the teacher, when appropriate.

Student performance information is easily accessible to the teacher.

Management system includes adequate security.

Program allows printout and screen display of student records.

Program can hold multiple performance records of a single class (e.g. 35 to 50 students).

Program can hold multiple performance records of several classes (e.g. up to 5 classes) arranged by class.

Documentation and Support Materials

Quality of packaging is durable and appropriate for student use (e.g. not too large to be used at a computer station).

Student, parent or teacher guides and materials are clearly identified as such.

Technical and operational explanations for implementation are clear and complete.

If appropriate, 'quick start-up' section is included.

Useful reproducible students' worksheets are provided.

Other valuable support materials are provided (e.g. wall charts).

Sample screen-by-screen printouts of the program are provided.

Teacher support materials can be separated from student materials.

Useful suggestions are provided for introductory classroom activities.

Useful suggestions are provided for classroom activities during the use of the program, where necessary or helpful.

Useful suggestions are provided for follow up activities.

Useful suggestions are given for classroom logistics in a variety of hardware situations (e.g. single or multiple machines) and student groupings.

Useful suggestions are provided on how to integrate program with the regular curriculum.

If the program is open-ended, subject-specific suggestions are included.

Clear explanations of the differences between the various difficulty levels are provided.

Prerequisite skills are clearly stated.

Accurate and clear descriptions of content topics are provided.

Where appropriate, a description of how material correlates to standard textbook series is provided.

Necessary information can be found quickly and easily (e.g. contains index, table of contents).

Quick reference card for program use is included, where appropriate.

Printed text is clear and readable.

Printed graphics are clear and readable.

Printed text is free of errors in spelling, grammar, punctuation and usage.

Technical Quality

Audio can be adjusted (i.e. turned down or off).

Audio is clear and used effectively.

Character sets used in text display are clear, appropriate, and visually interesting.

Graphics are acceptable on a monochrome monitor.

Graphics are clear and can be easily interpreted.

Program is 'crash-proof'.

Program runs consistently under all normal conditions and is 'bug-free'.

Program runs without undue delays (e.g. graphics fill in a timely manner, does not excessively access disc drive).

The transitions between screen displays are effective (e.g. text changes).

Program guards against multiple key presses advancing the student past the next screen (e.g. leaning on return key and thereby missing several screens as they flash by).

Program avoids unnecessary or inappropriate moving back and forth between screens (e.g. from page to feedback or data pages).

Special features (e.g. flash, inverse, scrolling, split screen) are used appropriately and effectively.

Program requires a minimal amount of typing (except typing programs).

Random generation or selection is used when appropriate (e.g. to allow repeated use by varying the problems or data presented).

Program judges responses accurately and accounts for minor variations in the format of the input (e.g. accepts either the correct word or letter choice in a multiple choice item).

Program allows user to correct answer before being accepted by the program.

Program accepts partial answers as correct whenever appropriate.

Where students must input responses, inappropriate keys are disabled.

Control keys are used consistently.

Students require a minimum amount of teacher supervision while using the program, when appropriate.

Computer (and peripherals) operation does not interfere with concentration on activity.

Program makes effective use of peripheral devices (e.g. joysticks) for alternate input modes while still allowing keyboard input.

Program considers a previously unexplored potential of the computer or greatly expands an existing capability (e.g. new animation techniques, digitized speech).

Program uses other technologies (e.g. audio cassette, videodisc, videotape) to enhance learning, when appropriate.

Printing is easy and simple to accomplish with a variety of popular printers.

Clarity

Procedural and instructional statements are clear.

On-screen prompts clearly indicate where user should focus attention.

Frame formatting is clear, uncluttered, and consistent from screen to screen (e.g. screen input is restricted to a consistent location).

Presentation of each discrete content topic is logical.

Sequence of content topics and instruction is logical and in appropriate steps.

Sequence of menu items is logical.

Prompts and cues are clear and consistently and logically applied.

Hints are clear and not misleading (e.g. length of spaces in fill-in blanks matches number of letters needed).

Demonstrations and examples are clear and available when appropriate.

Interface is simple enough to be used with little or no reading of the documentation.

Program makes clear where the user is in the program (e.g. question number, page headings).

User-computer communication is consistent and logical.

Prompts to save work are given when appropriate.

Start-up and Implementation

Teacher:

Software code modifications or unusual manipulations of discs are not
required to use program effectively.

Start-up time for teacher implementation is not excessive.

Teacher needs a minimum of computer competencies to operate program
(e.g. does not require installing add-on boards).

Student:

Start-up time for student implementation is brief enough to permit
completion of a lesson.

Students need a minimum of computer competencies to operate program (e.g. does not require use of control-key combinations).

Graphics and Audio

Graphics and audio are used to motivate.

Graphics and audio are appropriate for the intended student population.

Graphics, audio and color enhance the instructional process.

Graphics help focus attention to appropriate content and are not dis-
tracting.

Probeware and Peripherals Included in the Software Package

Probes or peripherals are durable.

Probes or peripherals are sensitive.

Audio and/or graphic quality are effective.

Probes or peripherals are easy to install.

Calibration is accurate and easy.

Data displays are flexible (e.g. can be scaled, redrawn).

Data analysis is useful.

Hardware and Marketing Issues

Potential usefulness of the program justifies its price in comparison to
other similar products.

Peripherals (not included in the package) that are difficult to acquire or
inappropriately expensive are not required.

Producer field test data are available.

Field test data indicate that students learned more or better, or had a
better attitude toward the subject matter, as a result of using the
program.

Preview copies are available.
Back-up copies are provided.
Adequate warranty is provided.
Telephone support is available.
If allowable, multiple loading is possible.
Site license is available.
Network versions are available.
Multiple copies discount available.

Appendix J
CD-ROM Selection Checklist (NCET, 1992)
Some Questions to Ask Before Purchasing CD-ROM

Which computer system will the disc run on?
Will your computer system do justice to the illustrations?
Is the operation by keyboard or mouse, or both?
Can we have the disc for a trial period?
Is the language and spelling on the disc Queen's English or American English?
How much bias is there in the content of the disc?
Is printing out easy and intuitive?
Can the selected material readily be down-loaded to disc?
Can subsections of the disc be searched?
Is the software to control the CD-ROM on the disc itself or is it supplied on a separate floppy disc?
Does the software manage memory resources well?
What search procedures are available?
What is the language level on the disc?
Is the user interface tolerant of typing and spelling errors?
Can you select exactly what you want to print out or save to disc?
Are there any supporting features?
Can the illustrations be printed out?
Can images be readily transferred?
Is there a sound capability to accompany the pictures?

Bibliography

ALDERSON, G., BLAKELEY, B., MILLWOOD, R. and DEANE, S. (1993) *Transformations*, Chepstow, AVP.

ALEXANDER, K. and BLANCHARD, D. (1985) *Educational Software: A Creator's Handbook*, Loughborough, Tecmedia.

ANDERSON, J. (1985) 'Software Evaluation', in ALEXANDER, K. and BLANCHARD, D. (Eds) *Educational Software: A Creator's Handbook*, Loughborough, Tecmedia, pp. 197–227.

ASTON, M. (1990) 'Mathematics — Jewel in the Computer Crown', in McDOUGALL, A. and DOWLING, C. (Eds) *Computers in Education*, Amsterdam, North-Holland, pp. 629–32.

BACON, S.J. (1981) 'Syllabuses for the Future', in LEWIS, R. and TAGG, E.D. (Eds) *Computers in Education*, Amsterdam, North-Holland, pp. 671–6.

BEECH, G. (1983) *Computer Based Learning: Practical Microcomputing Methods*, Wilmslow, Sigma Technical Press.

BENNETT, E. (1987) *Nuclides Database*, London, UKAEA.

BISHOP, P. (1993) 'Classroom Computers and the Role of the Primary Teacher', in KNIERZINGER, A. and MOSER, M. (Eds) *Informatics and Changes in Learning*, Linz, Austria, Institute for School and New Technology, III/5–8.

BITTER, G. and CAMUSE, R. (1988) *Using a Microcomputer in the Classroom*, Englewood Cliffs, NJ, Prentice-Hall.

BLEASE, D. (1986) *Evaluating Educational Software*, London, Croom Helm.

BLEASE, D. (1988) 'Choosing Educational Software', in JONES, A. and SCRIMSHAW, P. (Eds) *Computers in Education 5–13*, Milton Keynes, Open University Press, pp. 277–99.

BROWNELL, G. (1987) *Computers and Teaching*, St. Paul, Minnesota, West Publishing Company.

BURKHARDT, H., FRASER, R., CLOWES, M., EGGLESTON, J. and WELLS, C. (1982) *Design and Development of Programs as Teaching Material*, London, Council for Educational Technology.

BURT, C. (1985) 'Software in the Classroom — A Form for Teacher Use', *The Computing Teacher*, **12**, May, pp. 16–9.

CHANDLER, D. (1984) *Young Learners and the Microcomputer*, Milton Keynes, Open University Press.

CHATTERTON, J.L. (1985) 'Evaluating CAL in the Classroom', in REID, I. and RUSHTON, J. (Eds) *Teachers, Computers and the Classroom*, Manchester, Manchester University Press, pp. 88–95.

CLARKE, M. (1988) 'Mapwork Skills — Pupils' Experiences with L', *Journal of Computer Assisted Learning*, **4**, (3), pp. 182–4.

COBURN, P., KELMAN, P., ROBERTS, N., SNYDER, T., WATT, D. and WEINER, C. (1985) *Practical Guide to Computers in Education (Second Edition)*, Reading, Massachusetts, Addison-Wesley.

COOPER, Z. and RILEY, D. (1986) *Human Population Growth*, Chepstow, AVP.

COPE, P. and WALSH, T. (1990) 'Programming in Schools: 10 Years On', *Journal of Computer Assisted Learning*, **6**, (1), pp. 119–27.

COSGROVE, R.B. (1986) *Weather Report*, Brisbane, Department of Education, Queensland.

COX, R. and CUMMING, G. (1990) 'The Role of Exploration-Based Learning in the Development of Expertise', in McDOUGALL, A. and DOWLING, C. (Eds) *Computers in Education*, Amsterdam, North-Holland, pp. 359–64.

DEPARTMENT OF EDUCATION AND SCIENCE (1990) *Technology in the National Curriculum*, London, HMSO.

EDUCOM (1989) *Software Snapshots: Where Are You in the Picture?* Washington, DC, EDUCOM.

FLAVELL, H., GOMBERG, M. and SQUIRES, D. (1989) *TELETOM: A Telecommunications Adventure*, London, British Telecom Education Service.

FLAVELL, H., GOMBERG, M. and SQUIRES, D. (1993) *Priority*, London, British Telecom Education Service.

GAGNE, R.M. (1970) *The Conditions of Learning*, New York, Holt, Rinehart and Winston.

GRIFFEN, J. (1989) 'Hot Off the Press', *Times Educational Supplement*, p. 45.

HARRIS, J. (1985) *Revised Nuffield A-level Physics Pack*, Chepstow, AVP.

HECK, W., JOHNSON, J. and KANSKY, R. (1981) *Guidelines for Evaluating Computerized Instructional Materials*, Reston, Virginia, National Council for Teachers of Mathematics.

HELLER, R. (1991) 'Evaluating Software: A Review of the Options', *Computers and Education*, **17**, (4), pp. 285–91.

HEYDEMAN, M.T. and McCORMICK, S.J. (1982) *Enzyme Kinetics*, Chepstow, AVP.

HOFMEISTER, A. (1984) *Microcomputer Applications in the Classroom*, New York, Holt, Rinehart and Winston.

HOYLES, C., HEALY, L. and SUTHERLAND, R. (1991) 'Patterns of Discussion between Pupil Pairs in Computer and Non-Computer Environments', *Journal of Computer Assisted Learning*, **7**, (4), pp. 210–28.

ITMA COLLABORATION (1982) *Microcomputers in the Mathematics Classroom*, Harlow, Longmans.

JOHNSTON, V.M. (1987) 'The Evaluation of Microcomputer Programs: An Area of Debate', *Journal of Computer Assisted Learning*, **3**, (1), pp. 40–50.

KEMMIS, S., ATKIN, R. and WRIGHT, E. (1977) 'How Do Students Learn?' Working Papers on CAL, Occasional Paper No. 5, Centre for Applied Research in Education, University of East Anglia, UK.

KERNER, I.O. (1988) 'Mathematical Assessment of Courseware Efficiency', in LOVIS, F. and TAGG, E.D. (Eds) *Computers in Education: Proceedings of the European Conference on Computers in Education*, Amsterdam, North-Holland, pp. 651–6.

KIDD, M.E. and HOLMES, G. (1984) 'CAL Evaluation: A Cautionary Word', *Computers and Education*, **8**, (1), pp. 77–84.

KINNEAR, J. (1982) *Catlab*, CONDUIT.

KINNEAR, J. (1983) *Heredity Dog*, Science Education Resources Pty. Ltd.

KOMOSKI, P.K. (1987) 'Educational Microcomputer Software Evaluation', in MOONEN, J. and PLOMP, T. (Eds) *Eurit86: Developments in Educational Software and Courseware*, Oxford, Pergamon Press, pp. 399–404.

KOSEL, M. and FISH, M. (1983) *The Factory*, Pleasantville, NY, Sunburst Communications Inc.

KRAUSE, K. (1984) 'Choosing Computer Software that Works', *Journal of Reading*, 28, pp. 24–7.

LANGHORNE, M.J., DONHAM, J.O., GROSS, J.F. and REHMKE, D. (1989) *Teaching with Computers: A New Menu for the '90s*, London, Kogan Page.

LAWLER, R.W. (1985) *Computer Experience and Cognitive Development*, Chichester, Ellis Horwood.

LEWIS, R. (1986) 'Some Aspects of Classroom Processes', Occasional Paper ITE/12/86, Lancaster, University of Lancaster.

MACDONALD, B., ATKIN, R., JENKINS, D. and KEMMIS, S. (1977) 'Computer Assisted Learning: its Educational Potential', in HOOPER, R. (Ed) *Final*

Report of the Director National Development Programme in Computer Assisted Learning, London, Council for Educational Technology.

MALONE, T.W. (1981) 'Toward a Theory of Intrinsically Motivating Instruction', *Cognitive Science*, **4**, pp. 333–69.

MARCHANT, M. (1988) 'Collaborative Learning and L', *Journal of Computer Assisted Learning*, **4**, (4) pp. 244–7.

MATSON, M. (1984) *Flowers of Crystal*, Barnstaple, 4Mation Educational Resources.

McDOUGALL, A. (1980) *Computers and Post-Primary Education in Victoria: A Study of Needs*, Report to the Director General's Computer Policy Committee, Melbourne, Education Department of Victoria.

McDOUGALL, A. (1988) 'Children, Recursion and Logo Programming', Unpublished Ph. D. Thesis, Monash University.

McDOUGALL, A. (1990) 'Children, Recursion and Logo Programming: An Investigation of Papert's Conjecture about the Variability of Piagetian Stages in Computer-Rich Cultures', in McDOUGALL, A. and DOWLING, C. (Eds) *Computers in Education*, Amsterdam, North-Holland, pp. 415–8.

McDOUGALL, A. and SQUIRES, D. (1986) 'Student Control in Computer Based Learning Environments', in SALVAS, A.D. and DOWLING, C. (Eds) *Computers in Education: On the Crest of a Wave?*, Melbourne, Computer Education Group of Victoria, pp. 269–72.

McGRAW HILL (1992) '*The Multimedia Encyclopedia of Mammalian Biology*', Maidenhead, McGraw Hill.

MicroSIFT (1982) *Evaluator's Guide for Microcomputer-Based Instructional Packages*, Eugene, Oregon, The International Council for Computers in Education.

MILLER, L. and BURNETT, J.D. (1986) 'Theoretical Considerations in Selecting Language Arts Software', *Computers and Education*, **10**, (1), pp. 159–65.

MILLER, P. (1993) 'The Multimedia Encyclopedia of Mammalian Biology: a Review', *The CTISS File*, **15**, pp. 21–4.

MINISTERS OF EDUCATION, CANADA (1985) *Software Evaluation*, Toronto, Council of Ministers of Education, Canada.

MOSS, G.D. (1992) 'Comparing Awareness and Use of Content-Free Software in Comprehensive Schools', *Computers and Education*, **18**, (4), pp. 283–91.

NCET (1992a) *Choosing and Using Portable Computers*, Coventry, National Council for Educational Technology.

NCET (1992b) *CD-ROM in Schools Scheme Evaluation Report*, Coventry, National Council for Educational Technology.

NEWMAN, J. (1988) 'Software Libraries: The Backbone of Schools' Computing', *Proceedings of the Australian Computer Education Conference*, Perth, Educational Computing Association of Western Australia, pp. 242–51.

NORMAN, D. (1983) 'Some Observations on Mental Models', in GENTNER, D. and STEVENS, A. (Eds) *Mental Models*, Hillsdale, New Jersey, Lawrence Erlbaum Associates Inc., pp. 7–14.

O'SHEA, B. (1988) 'DARTS', *Journal of Computer Assisted Learning*, **4**, (1), pp. 47–50.

O'SHEA, T. and SELF, J. (1983) *Learning and Teaching with Computers*, Brighton, The Harvester Press.

OECD (1989) *Information Technologies in Education: The Quest for Quality Software*, Paris, Organization for Economic Co-operation and Development.

OTA (1988) *Power On! New Tools for Teaching and Learning*, Washington, DC, US Government Printing Office.

OGBORN, J. (1985) *Dynamic Modelling System*, Chepstow, AVP.

PAPERT, S. (1980a) 'Computer-Based Microworlds as Incubators for Powerful Ideas', in TAYLOR, R. (Ed) *The Computer in the School: Tutor, Tool, Tutee*, New York, Teachers College Press.

PAPERT, S. (1980b) *Mindstorms*, Brighton, Harvester Press.

PEA, R. (1987) 'LOGO and Problem Solving', in SCANLON, E. and O'SHEA, T. (Eds) *Educational Computing*, Chichester, John Wiley, pp. 155–160.

PELGRUM, J. and PLOMP, T. (1991) *The Use of Computers Worldwide*, Oxford, Pergamon Press.

PENTER, K. (1981) 'Computers in Elementary and Secondary Schools in Western Australia', in LEWIS, R. and TAGG, E.D. (Eds) *Computers in Education*, Amsterdam, North-Holland, pp. 603–9.

POOLE, A. (1988) 'Working with DEVTRAY', *Journal of Computer Assisted Learning*, **4**, (3), pp. 173–6.

PREECE, J. and JONES, A. (1985) 'Training Teachers to Select Educational Software: Results of a Formative Evaluation of an Open University Pack', *British Journal of Educational Technology*, **16**, (1), pp. 9–20.

PREECE, J. and SQUIRES, D. (1984) 'Helping Teachers to Recognise Quality Software', *Computer Education*, February, pp. 20–1.

PRESTON, C. and SQUIRES, D. (1989) *Newsnet*, London, British Telecom Education Service.

RAJARATNAM, M. (1988) 'WRITE with a Purpose', *Journal of Computer Assisted Learning*, **4**, (1), pp. 44–7.

RAWITSCH, D. (1983) 'Educational Courseware', in SALVAS, A.D. (Ed) *Could*

You Use a Computer? Melbourne, Computer Education Group of Victoria, pp. 345–7.

REAY, D.G. (1985) 'Evaluating Educational Software for the Classroom', in REID, I. and RUSHTON, J. (Eds) *Teachers, Computers and the Classroom*, Manchester, Manchester University Press, pp. 79–87.

REID, I. (1985) 'So Far, So Good . . .', in REID, I. and RUSHTON, J. (Eds) *Teachers, Computers and the Classroom*, Manchester, Manchester University Press, pp. 184–95.

RIDGWAY, J., BENZIE, D., BURKHARDT, H., COUPLAND, J., FIELD, G., FRASER, R. and PHILLIPS, R. (1984) 'Conclusions from Catastrophes', *Computers and Education*, **8**, (1), pp. 93–100.

ROGERS, J.B. and AUSTING, R.H. (1981) 'Computer Science in Secondary Schools: Recommendations for a One-Year Course', in LEWIS, R. and TAGG, E.D. (Eds) *Computers in Education*, Amsterdam, North-Holland, pp. 651–6.

ROWNTREE, D. (1982) *Educational Technology in Curriculum Development*, London, Harper and Row.

SALVAS, A.D. and THOMAS, G.J. (1984) *Evaluation of Software*, Melbourne, Education Department of Victoria.

SAUNDERS, M. and GROSLER, W. (1990) 'The MEDA Project: Developing Evaluation Competence in the Training Software Domain', in NORRIE, D.H. and SIX, H.W. (Eds) *Lecture Notes in Computer Science 438*, New York, Springer Verlag, pp. 288–300.

SCHALL, W.E., LEAKE, L. and WHITAKER, W. (1986) '*Computer Education: Literacy and Beyond*', Monterey, California, Brooks-Cole.

SCHWARTZ, J., YERUSHALMY, M., and GORDON, M. (1985) *The Geometric Supposer*, Pleasantville, NY, Sunburst Communications.

SELF, J. (1985) *Microcomputers in Education: a Critical Appraisal of Educational Software*, Brighton, Harvester Press.

SEWELL, D.F. (1990) *New Tools for New Minds*, New York, Harvester Wheatsheaf.

SHINGLES, D. (1988) 'How Do You Know What You're Getting?' *Proceedings of the Australian Computer Education Conference*, Perth, Educational Computing Association of Western Australia, pp. 332–9.

SHUTE, V.J. and GLASER, T.R. (1990) 'A Large-Scale Evaluation of an Intelligent Discovery World: Smithtown', *Interactive Learning Environments*, **1**, (1), pp. 51–77.

SIMONSON, R. and THOMPSON, A. (1990) *Educational Computing Foundations*, New York, Macmillan.

SKINNER, B.F. (1938) *The Behaviour of Organisms: and Experimental Analysis*, Appleton-Century-Crofts.

SLOANE, H., GORDON, H., GUNN, C. and MICKELSEN, V. (1989) *Evaluating Educational Software: A Guide for Teachers*, Englewood Cliffs, NJ, Prentice-Hall.

SMITH, D. and KEEP, R. (1988) 'Eternal Triangulation: Case Studies in the Evaluation of Educational Software by Classroom-Based Teacher Groups', *Computers and Education*, **12**, (1), pp. 151–6.

SOFTWARE PRODUCTION ASSOCIATES (undated) *Newspaper*, Leamington Spa, Software Production Associates.

SQUIRES, D. (1981) 'Environmental Studies and Computer Assisted Learning', in LEWIS, R. and TAGG, D. (Eds) *Computers in Education*, Amsterdam. North-Holland, pp. 27–32.

SQUIRES, D. (1985) 'Planning a Motorway: Making CAL Work in Today's Classrooms', in TAGG, W. (Ed) *A Parent's Guide to Educational Software*, London, Telegraph Publications, pp. 65–73.

SQUIRES, D. and McDOUGALL, A. (1986) 'Computer Based Microworlds: A Definition to Aid Design', *Computer Education*, **10**, (3), pp. 375–8.

SQUIRES, D. and WATSON, D. (1983) *Motorway Route*, Chepstow, AVP.

STAKE, B. (1991) 'PLATO Mathematics: The Teacher and Fourth Grade Students Respond', in BLOMEYER, R. and MARTIN, D. (Eds) *Case Studies in Computer Aided Learning*, London, The Falmer Press, pp. 53–109.

STRAKER, A. (1990) *Young Children and Computers*, Oxford, Blackwell.

SUPPES, P. (1967) 'The Teacher and Computer-Assisted Instruction', in TAYLOR, R. (Ed) (1980) *The Computer in the School: Tutor, Tool, Tutee*, New York, Teachers College Press.

TAGG, W. (Ed) (1985) *A Parent's Guide to Educational Software*, London, Telegraph Publications.

TAYLOR, R.P. (Ed) (1980) *The Computer in the School: Tutor, Tool, Tutee*, New York, Teachers College Press.

TEMPLETON, R. (1985) 'Be Careful but Don't Worry: A Guide to Buying Educational Software', in TAGG, W. (Ed) *A Parent's Guide to Educational Software*, London, Telegraph Publications, pp. 54–64.

THOMPSON, D. (1985) 'Evaluating Computer Programs', in CHANDLER, D. and MARCUS, S. (Eds) *Computers and Literacy*, Milton Keynes, Open University Press.

UNDERWOOD, J.D.M. and UNDERWOOD, G. (1990) *Computers and Learning*, Oxford, Blackwell.

VICTORIAN CURRICULUM and ASSESSMENT BOARD (1989) *Information Technology Study Design*, Melbourne, Victorian Curriculum and Assessment Board.

WADDINGTON, D. and WIGLEY, P. (1985) 'Support materials for *Counter*', in *Micros in Maths Inservice Pack*, Hatfield, Microelectronics Education Programme.

WATSON, D. (1986) *Palestine 1947*, Chepstow, AVP.

WATSON, D. (1987) *Developing CAL: Computers in the Curriculum*, London, Harper and Row.

WATSON, D. (Ed) (1993) *The ImpacT Report*, London, King's College London.

WATSON, D., MOORE, A. and RHODES, V. (1993) 'Case Studies', in WATSON, D. (Ed) (*1993*) *The ImpacT Report*, London, King's College London, pp. 61–96.

WEBB, M. (Ed) (1991) *Model Builder*, Hatfield, Advisory Unit for Computer Education.

WEIR, S. (1987) *Cultivating Minds*, New York, Harper and Row.

WELLINGTON, J.J. (1985) *Children, Computers and the Curriculum*, New York, Harper and Row.

WIGLEY, D. (1985) *Counter*, Hatfield, Microelectronics Education Programme.

WILLS, S. (1986) *The First Fleet Convicts*, Melbourne, Edsoft.

WILLS, S., BUNNETT, A. and DOWNES, T. (1985) 'Convicts and Bushrangers: Educational Data Bases Brought Alive', in RASMUSSEN, B. (Ed) *The Information Edge: The Future for Educational Computing*, Brisbane, Computer Education Group of Queensland, pp. 117–26.

WINSHIP, J. (1988) 'Software Review or Evaluation: Are They Both Roses Or Is One A Lemon?', *Proceedings of the Australian Computer Education Conference*, Perth, Educational Computing Association of Western Australia, pp. 364–76.

WISHART, J. (1989) 'Cognitive Factors Related to User Involvement with Computers and their Effects upon Learning from an Educational Computer Game', unpublished paper presented at CAL89 conference.

WOODHOUSE, D. and McDOUGALL, A. (1986) *Computers: Promise and Challenge in Education*, Melbourne, Blackwell Scientific Publications.

Acknowledgments

The authors and publishers gratefully acknowledge the following:

The table on page 64 is taken from *Young Learners and the Microcomputers*, by Chandler, D. published in (1984), The Open University Press and is reproduced here with the permission of the publishers.

The quotation on page 147 is taken from *CD-ROM in Schools Scheme: an evaluation report*, by Steadman, S. Nash, C. and Eurat, M. (Eds) 1992 by the National Council for Educational Technology and is reproduced here with the permission of the publishers.

The quotation on page 127 is reprinted from *Computers in Education*, 10(1), Miller, L. and Burnett, J.D., Theoretical Considerations in Selecting Language Arts Software (1986), with kind permission from Pergamon Press Ltd, Headington Hall, Oxford OX3 0BW, UK.

The quotation on pages 139–147 is taken from *Power On! New Tools for Teaching and Learning* by the US Congress, Office of Technology Assessment published in 1992 by the US Government Printing Office.

The quotation on pages 130–134 is reprinted from 'Evaluating Educational Software for the Classroom' *in Teachers, Computers and the Classroom* (Eds Reid, I. and Rushton, J.) by Reay, D.G. published in 1985 by Manchester University Press with kind permission of the author.

The quotations on page 37 and pages 134–139 are taken from *Evaluating Educational Software* by Blease, D. in 1984 by Croom Helm and are reproduced here with the permission of the publishers.

The quotation on pages 128–129 is taken from *Practical Guide to Computers in Education* by Coburn, P., Kelman, P., Roberts, N., Snyder, T., Watt, D. and Weiner, C. published in 1985 by the Addison-Wesley Publishing Company.

The quotations on pages 34–35 and pages 121–125 are reprinted from *Evaluator's Guide for Micro-computer-Based Instructional Packages* published in 1982 by MicroSIFT, International Council for Computers in Education, c/o Department of Computer and Information Science, University of Oregon, with kind permission of the publishers.

The quotation on page 134 is taken from 'Be Careful but Don't Worry: A Guide to Buying Educational Software' by Templeton, R. in *A Parent's Guide to Educational Software.* Tagg, W. (Ed) published in 1985 by Telegraph Publications.

The quotation on page 129 is taken from *Micros in Schools (P541)* produced and written by The Open University in 1984 and is reproduced here with the permission of the publishers.

The quotations on pages 32–33 and pages 134, 126–127 are taken from *Evaluation of Software* by Salvas, A.D. and Thomas, G.J. published in 1984 by the Education Department of Victoria.

Index